The Mighty Woman's Adventures Abroad

Short story collections and other fiction available from Evertype

The Mighty Woman's Adventures Abroad
(Art de Creag, tr. Mícheál Ó hAodha 2020)

Letter from my Foster Mother and other stories
(Fionntán de Brún, tr. Mícheál Ó hAodha 2020)

The Scarlet Petal and other stories
(Ryan Petrie 2021)

The Book of Poison (Panu Petteri Höglund & S. Albert Kivinen,
tr. Colin Parmer & Tino Warinowski 2014)

The Partisan and other Stories (Gabriel Rosenstock,
tr. Mícheál Ó hAodha & Gabriel Rosenstock 2014)

A Nosegay of Pleasant Delights: Five-minute fictions (Brian S. Lee 2012)

The Burning Woman and other stories (Frank Roger 2012)

Neighbours: Stories in Mennonite Low German and English
Nohbasch: Jeschichte opp Plautdietsch enn Enjlisch
(Jack Thiessen 2014)

Nosy Neighbours: Stories in Mennonite Low German and English
Nieschieaje Nohbasch: Jeschichte opp Plautdietsch enn Enjlisch
(Jack Thiessen 2015)

The Mighty Woman's Adventures Abroad

A novel by
Art de Creag

Translated from the Irish by
Mícheál Ó hAodha

e

evertype
2020

Published by Evertype, 19ᴀ Corso Street, Dundee, ᴅᴅ2 1ᴅʀ, Scotland. www.evertype.com.

First published in Irish by Coiscéim, Baile Átha Cliath, 1995, with the title *Eachtra na Mná Móire thar Lear*.

A catalogue record for this book is available from the British Library.

ISBN-10 1-78201-228-1
ISBN-13 978-1-78201-228-3

Set in Minion Pro and Étienne by Michael Everson.

Cover: Mathew Staunton, The Onslaught Press.

Contents

Foreword

Who else would praise my efforts if I didn't do so myself?

This work of high literature is a fiction from beginning to end other than those damned fools who encouraged me to write this novel in order to torment and make a mockery of all the most noble Gaels of the country. There is no incident in this book that relates to any creature, living or dead, whether man, woman or child and I was never in any of the places mentioned in this story either.

That said, I have to acknowledge a number of Irish Gaels whom I have always held in high regard and who are guilty as charged seeing as they felt that this work was worth publishing, having read the first draft of it. I have the proof to demonstrate that Pádraig Ó Snodaigh and Alan Titley can be counted amongst the guilty on this score. I'm probably as well off including a list of all the culprits here:

Áine Nic Gearailt
Pádraigín Ní Mhurchú
The people of Annaghmakerrig, Co. Monaghan
Máire Nic Fhionnachtaigh
Brian Ó Maoileoin
Micheál Ó Maoileoin
Pádraig Ó Murchú
Breandán Ó Mearáin

Pádraig Mac Giolla Ruaidh
Gearóid Ó Cairealláin and the staff of *Lá*
Cathal Ó Donnghaile
Colm Mac Aindreasa
Seán Mac Aindreasa
Séamas Mag Fhionnaile
Eoghan Ó Néill

It was no easy task to shape this novel in order to make it presentable to the literati of Ireland/

For a long time it looked as if this project was heading for a slow lingering death in truth. Or that it would prove the tune that killed off the old cow or the straw that broke the camel's back I'd like to take this opportunity however to thank from the depths of my heart every woman who kissed me during that tumultuous part of my life I spent working on the book and also every man who stood me a pint at the time, before that, or even after that too. May everyone who died before they could see the fruits of this effort in our native literature and language come to fruition rest in peace.

Eternal peace to all of to all of them and to you dear reader who may now read this story.

Art de Creag
Belfast 1995

Part 1

Chapter 1

Whenever I feel lonely here in Dublin city, I think back on how lovely it would be to find myself sitting back in front of big turf fire in the wilds of County Leitrim? And what would I be doing there, you might ask? What else, but listening to my grandmother giving out stink to my Uncle Maurice about something or other. Either that, or the pair of them knocking strips off my Uncle Philip, a member of the family who was usually absent.

Dear readers, blood is thicker than water and *briseann an dúchas trí shúile an chait*[1]—heredity breaks out in the eyes of the cat—and you can't make a silk purse out of a sow's ear. For respectable people—the likes of yourselves—there's a good chance that there are people in this life and if you didn't know anything about them at all, it wouldn't bother you and you'd be better off. Consequently, it's better that I tell you a bit about myself, in case you assume that I belong to some class of people you're not too fond of. You're entitled to know who I am and who I belong to; this won't take long either seeing as I don't have too many relations anyway. I have just my two uncles and my granny, that's it.

---

1   *Briseann an dúchas trí shúile an chait*—'Heredity breaks out in the eyes of the cat.' An old Gaelic proverb that indicates that the nature vs. nurture argument has been going on for centuries with this proverb siding with those on the nature side of the debate – i.e. the cat's instinct for cruelty and savagery and man's propensity for same.

I can't help being clannish at the end of the day. The way I look at things is: if God ordained it that there were just three others in the world who were close relatives of mine, it's logical that all of my attention is on them. I've never laid eyes on my father and I can barely remember my mother. But it was in my mother's house that I was born and reared by my granny. And my granny and two uncles were the only family that I ever had, my Uncle Maurice who lived with us, and my Uncle Philip who didn't. Just the four of us, linked together like the four-hand reel or the four-leaved clover—and this was my entire world for many years. And whenever I heard people say that my granny had the sharpest tongue in that part of the country, I'd swell with pride the same as any child who hears rare and unusual traits ascribed to their relatives.

Chapter 2

When I was small I was very small. If my grandmother sent me to the shop whenever it was busy, I might be there all day before the shopkeeper noticed me and by then, I'd have forgotten what I'd gone to buy there to buy in the first place. I'd know exactly why I'd been sent there on first arrival, but having listened to the chat of the other customers for a few hours, it'd all have disappeared from my mind—only to be replaced by all the wonderful gossip and news I'd heard there.

I might have been small then but I had big ears all the same! And even if I returned home with an empty basket, at least my head was full of stories and that was worth something. Because as my granny often told me, I was a better storyteller or raconteur than anyone on the radio! Maybe granny was being sarcastic when she said this—particularly when I came home from the shop without anything—my only provisions consisting of a series of gossip and rumours doing the rounds. When all is said and done, I think that my grandmother preferred my take on the parish news than anyone else's. The disadvantage of my insights—as compared to those of other people—was that I usually had all the rumours mixed in through the day's news— that I'd have made links between issues that others hadn't. The way my grandmother saw it anyway—this left international issues far more pleasant and comprehensible than before!

If Big Andy's dog was missing for two weeks, this undoubtedly related to the expansion of communism across the country. The price of tea and tobacco constantly rising was connected in some way to that huge, black monster-shape that'd Joe Anthony had spotted passing over the peak of the hill on a Sunday night. No wonder Nora from the Bottom of the Lake's goat kept breaking out onto the road on her?

Wasn't Nora's cousin training for the priesthood and her nephew joining the army? There was no denying it either but that the war in South America had put Red Paddy back on the drink again.

And what else could it have been—only the Chinese opening a new restaurant in Dublin every week—this must've been why Mickey Dan's ram had just dropped dead in the field one day? This was how I brought the day's news home from the shop anyway. When it came to reporters and news-people, I was always breaking new ground—always, always.

Chapter 3

When I was small, I was so small that I could sit in the company of a handful of women in the house or in the shop without anyone noticing that I was there at all. As I say, I had big ears and I didn't miss a trick.

The thing that always surprised me most listening to the women was how much time they spent discussing the institution of marriage. It was clear that they knew the ins and outs of every marriage made in that area for years and years. Unsurprisingly, this set my child's mind reflecting on the same topic.

"Granny! Haven't I two uncles?"

"You do indeed love? And God help them."

"But Granny! How come they're not married?"

I might have been small but I'd noticed that this subject was quite a heavy and serious one—the difference between these two different stations in life i.e. the single state and the married state. And it was a source of curiosity and surprise to me why neither of them had given this second state in life a go. It was as if they'd managed to elude this side of life completely and slipped their way around it. As quick as the early train from Sligo to Dublin sped past, without so much as a bye-your-leave to the flat open terrain of County Leitrim. The by-pass of marriage my Uncle Philip had never travelled down and the path of love my Uncle Maurice had never wandered either. And you'd have thought that there must have been times when the springs of youth had resounded within them and they'd have considered changing their status—surely? It had never happened however. The years came and went and neither of them seemed to notice the passing of the seasons. The desire for procreation of the squirrels, the night-eels slithering across the fields in search of love or the budding of the trees. Such inclinations never reverberated in both men at all. The arrival and passing of the breeding season, they never noticed.

"But Granny! How come they never married?"

"Arah, love! Sure, who'd have them? Who'd walk down the aisle with either of those fellows?"

Young as I was, I understood that the marriage of either of my uncles would prove a rare and unlikely event.

Chapter 4

When I was small, I was happy enough to be small. Recognizing the great advantages of being small is how I spent my time—that and learning how life works, slowly but surely. Many's the small creature that can go somewhere where the big one can't follow them and there are many other major advantages to being small also. The good things never last too long in this life. And the same goes for being small too. We grow, we change, we develop. Not that our development coincides step-by-step with our growth either. If growth in my case led to some new developments in my life, it didn't lead to much in the way of improvement, that's for sure! When I was small, my troubles were far smaller than me. But gradually, as I grew taller, my worries and troubles increased until they were like a great wall of sky all around me.

Of course, you could say that these are common and everyday problems in the lives of any child—particularly the first one that I came up against—the problem of my First Starting School—but anyway! And it was my sudden growth spurt that was the cause of that too! It seemed to me that one day I was small and the next, people were telling me:

"Hey, Little Packie, but haven't you got big?"

and

"God, but no-one's ever seen anyone grow up as quick as that little orphan-stray that Big Maggie's raising, have they?"

and

"That's a disgrace that the lanky yoke living down in Big Maggie's house hasn't been sent up the road to school with the other kids yet, isn't it?"

This type is talk had gone on for a while and my granny had ignored it for the most part. To give her her due, she'd never had much time for schooling or education anyway. My Uncle Maurice agreed with her for the most part on this question too. Except that he also knew the local authorities would have something to say about it.

"They'll set the law on you for not sending him to school mother."

"May the devil roast them on the hot coals of hell—themselves and their stupid laws!"

"But the neighbours might report us, mam?"

"Sure, I know well that most of them are the seed and breed of old informers? The neighbours! The only thing they care about is that the poor lad is consigned to the same level of stupidity and foolishness as their own little crawlers!"

My Uncle Philip, as expected, was the most vocal in recommending I get an education.

"If you don't send the child to school, he'll never get a job when he's older."

That was Uncle Maurice cutting across Philip as was his way.

"How do you know whether he'll ever find himself looking for a job, good, bad or indifferent, when he grows up anyway?"

My granny was of similar mind to Uncle Maurice when it came to schooling and employment, except that she knew that she had responsibilities in this regard, a fact that only made her hate the system more. She'd give me a pat with her hand and look at me and say: "If it ever comes down to it, Little Packie, if the day ever comes that I'm not here, any dealer or farmer would hire you for work come fair-day."

Anyway, the decision was eventually made to tip me head-first into the pool of education. If I refer to it as a pool, it is not such a bad metaphor really. Because I felt as if I'd been thrown into it without any safety ring. Flung into the water and beset by all sorts of starving fish, cannibalistic and ferocious!

So this was the position I found myself in for a while—until I realized that I had been neither drowned nor destroyed. By then, I had a different metaphor for this place of education. I saw it now as a battlefield, a place where I'd no option but to follow the rules of war as ordained there and to adapt myself to them in order to survive; and there was no safer place than school either if you found yourself in a position that you assumed charge of the whole place, was there? But that's another story again. Another chapter altogether.

Chapter 5

The townie often thinks that it's easy to be a big shot in a small village. It's not that easy really, as it happens. I know this better than most as I'm one of the people who've managed this feat. And me—just a kid in short pants too—not that I found it easy by any means!

During my early days at school, I wasn't exactly known for being cool, calm and collected by the other kids. In fact, you could tell by me that I was a born coward from the day I was born. They say a quick run is better than a bad stand however, don't they?

And I always preferred to run for it than make any stand at all—good, bad or different. It's true that my ability for gobbing spits at someone when they weren't looking was well-recognized. Other than that, I rarely involved myself in any fracas or fight unless it was to try and stop one! I was no hero at the best of times. I never willingly took on heights or climbed trees or high walls, and I was afraid of every shadow come nightfall. The sound of a dog barking, big or small, was enough to send the heart crossways in me.

But if I was so frightened and cowardly at first, how did I eventually blossom into someone the whole community looked up to, you might ask? It was by accident and a stroke of good luck (or bad luck) that this happened. I don't deserve the credit for it either. It was the young kids in the school who pushed the glory my way and made a big deal of me despite my best efforts! Ironically enough, as things turned out, it was the fact I was happy to push *others* around and walk all over them that helped me rise to the top.

Not that this happened overnight either, it goes without saying. You might say to me that this makes no sense, but I'll tell you why now. Because life itself is one big contradiction, isn't it true for me? Because if I'd stayed that small puny little creature whose sole aim was avoiding risk and danger, I'd never have been crowned a big fish in the end. If I hadn't been a pathetic loser without an inch of courage or backbone, I'd never have gone anywhere and no-one would have thought anything of me! And that's the absolute truth!

And here's how it happened too.

The other children around me weren't slow to recognize the weakness in me. And once my classmates in national school copped on to how adept and able a coward I was, they looked to taunt and torment me about it mercilessly—every single day. Given my strong predilection for self-preservation, they got great fun out of trying to scare the hell out of me. The way they saw it—if I was sworn to cowardliness, then it was their job to constantly force me into a situation of mortal danger, every chance the devil gave their small malicious hearts. There was no better source of amusement they could ask for—come a fine summer's day or a long winter's night—but to tease me constantly. And this is how things were with me in my early schooldays.

A big lanky neighbouring lad was giving me a very hard time one day—just for a bit of fun for himself. The same lad was two years older than me, a half-stone heavier, and a foot higher taller. For one split second, I spotted my chance and even if I was absolutely petrified and disheartened, I grabbed it—I took the chance that the Good God and his Blessed Mother granted me and I clobbered your man with a powerful punch that sent him reeling. I hit him so hard that I stunned him and he found himself stretched out on the ground for a while. Once he recovered and got to his feet, he ran home crying. Did you think that they left me alone after that? If you think that, dear reader, you are as deluded as I was back then.

Chapter 6

Word of this great event spread through the village, the consequences of which were the exact opposite of what might've been expected. Because I had altered the normal course of events entirely! It's rare enough that life changes for the better and before long, I realized that it'd be me who was in trouble in this new scenario. And that I'd have been far better off if I hadn't struck that fateful blow on the lanky lad at all in the first place. In hindsight, and based on what followed afterwards, I wouldn't have minded one bit if the children had returned to their teasing and mocking of me as before.

All of this was water under the bridge for the moment however. It was as if none of these other things had ever happened to me at all. Instead of tormenting me as they'd done previously, a big crowd of small kids followed me everywhere now— all of them on a mission to find someone who'd prove my match as a fighter. They were obsessed now with finding lads for me to take on, fellas who were big enough and proud enough, and foolish enough to take me on—so that this crowd following me around now were inciting opponents against me and challenging them on my behalf!

And that wasn't all of it either.

Because an issue had arisen now amongst all of the children who were the same weight, age or size as the boy that I'd clocked, an issue that had never arisen before.

In view of the way I'd knocked that lanky lad spark out, anyone who thought highly of his fame and honour as a fighting man had to take me on now too and have a go. They were all obliged now to challenge me, one after another, and prove themselves in single combat against me.

Dear friends, this was a grim and dark period in my life, I can tell you! I was fighting now from one end of the week to the next, and there was no escaping it for the next 18 months! So that I became fiercer and dirtier in my fighting, at the same time as I emerged victorious from every encounter. And when the day came around that I'd beaten every kid in the village up to sixth class, my backers started importing strangers from places outside to fight me. In case I got soft or became unfit or anything! They began scouring the local villages and towns to find new opponents for me! By now, I realized that it was well past time for me to try and extricate myself from the trap I found myself in—all as a consequence of the courage that thrives in the terrified soul. This same courageous terror was tearing my heart out all the while that my supporters were combing the countryside looking for new opponents for me. If you'd seen some of the giants they brought in from the mountains to me! I'd be frightened out of my wits at the sight of these colossal, young bruisers and ironically, it was the same terror and fear that helped me beat them. I tore into them and fought them like a wild animal captured in a net. Until, eventually, I refused to suffer any more of it.

Well, there you go, my friends—this is how I managed to become a big shot in my home village while still just a schoolboy.

Chapter 7

And the consequences of all of this—would you believe it? Adults used to come up to me in school for a chat and to ask my advice on important and serious questions—questions relating to land, crops, livestock and weather. One big fishing man amongst them refused to go to the lake until he'd enquired with me beforehand about lines, baits and hooks. Even elderly and pious women used to consult me about devotional issues and prayer.

All of this confused me greatly—it goes without saying. Other than what I knew by then about street fighting, rucking, and general thuggery, I was as ignorant as an old plank of timber about most things.

Still, I had status.

Even if I had a name now as a dangerous buck, people still felt it worthwhile looking for my advice as relating to every aspect of life. This was around the same time as the Baroness from Germany arrived to fill the post as teacher in our local school. I hesitate to say it but this is the truth. We had things really good in that school prior to her arrival.

The teacher we had before her was a nice elderly man, and an understanding teacher. On recognizing that the lads who were in the last year at school showed me respect, even lads who were smaller and younger than me, he was quite happy to leave the entire administration of the school to me. And let me tell you that this was a good arrangement both for him and us. All the teaching was left up to him needless to say. But the children ran everything else for him. One girl took his shirts away to wash them for him. Another small girl again kept an eye out for the arrival of the parish priest on his behalf. One boy delivered his messages for him and another took care of his football coupons. A very able lad looked after the distilling side of things for him. Another fellow was responsible for warning us of any official visitors that might be on their way to the school and he was in trouble if he didn't warn us in time. From an administrative point of view, we had the best school in Ireland. Or, at least, that's how things were until the drink got the upper hand on the old master and a new teacher arrived who was as different from him as the cat is from the coach. A female teacher, a foreigner teacher, a teacher from Germany! As the old proverb goes—a new brush sweeps everything clean but the old brush knows every nook in the house.

Chapter 8

My Uncle Maurice spent time working abroad. Between working on the boats and on the docks and in the factories across the big cities of Britain, he was abroad for a year or two altogether. I asked him about it.

"Too much trouble," he says. "The people living in those cities are forever arguing and roaring at one another. They see any bit of peace or quiet as their earthly enemy."

"Was that why you came home?"

"Yes. After I'd travelled through the country over there a few times, I felt happy enough to come home again and to sit at my fire and relax. The worst tongue-lashing that your grandmother could give me was nothing after all of that!

My Uncle Philip was a different type. He had his own place out on the Main Road, called "VALLEYWORE SERVICES," that included a shop and a garage. He was a very go-ahead man, Philip and only rarely called into us, at his mother's house out in Manslaughter Hollow. If it wasn't that everyone knew our family history in the area already, I think he probably would've ignored us altogether. "I am 'VALLEYWORE SERVICES,' he'd often say to people. As much as to say that this was his surname really!

People used to say about my granny that she was as old as Iron Mountain but she'd always run anyone who advised her to apply for the old-age pension. "Government money!" she'd say. Who'd have any luck with the likes of that! It makes no odds what government is in, it's always blood money!"

My Uncle Morris said that he felt this was going over the top a bit but that my granny was entitled to her opinion all this same. This wasn't how my Uncle Philip saw things however. Money that Granny was entitled to from the state and she wouldn't accept it! It tormented him from one week to the next; the thought of it was actually shortening his time on this earth.

As regards my two uncles, it was no easy life trying to keep both of them sweet. You might as well have tried to split yourself in two. The people encounter one another, but the hills never meet—as the old proverb goes. By the wall at the church, once a week, was when my two uncles met one another. They'd often start off pleasant enough with one another and my Uncle Philip enquiring about my mother. But it never took long for the talk to switch to public affairs and before you knew it, an argument would break out between them. And if, like me, you were standing on the other side of the road—where the women and children usually stood—you could watch them go at it. Their two sticks raised in the air and they waving them at each other in threatening fashion. Next thing, you'd hear a man's voice above the crowd across the way—"Hey! Hey! Hey!" and "Ah… now lads! Now! Now!" Or maybe "Ah… for God's sake! Philip! Maurice! Remember where you are now, will you!"

You'd hear the women calling over:

"Outside the church as well! You two should be ashamed of yourselves."

Chapter 9

As villages and townlands disappear from our lives (a fact of history today) the time comes when the living link between the people and their community is broken—so that they are no longer a parish, a community, or a people anymore. One can see this just by looking at the changing appearance of the countryside. You mightn't see it at first glance but you'd certainly see it on a second one. Even if the houses line up along the edge of the road, as before, they have changed. Suddenly, the houses are the same as the telegraph poles. They have become part of the road. They show what direction the road is going in, the same as the poles. Where the road once followed the houses to service them nowadays, the road follows the houses as if to justify their existence. When you look at them now, you realize that everything has to go in the one direction from now on. Our parish was divided into two parts, our side with Fugitive's Wood and Manslaughter Pool while, on the other, lay the main road leading to Dublin. My Uncle Philip lived over there on the Main Road side as it was known. Both halves of the parish had no time for one another for some reason. Every now and then, my granny would send me over to Uncle Philip's place with a note asking him for a loan of some money. I don't know whether these loans were ever paid back but sometimes I felt as if I was the one paying for them seeing as I had to listen to all of Uncle Philip's opinions while I was over there.

Returning from "VALLEYMORE SERVICES" with the money for my granny in a sealed envelope, my Uncle Philip's words would still be ringing in my ears. "What's the point in going against the tide of life? We need to move with the times… Everyone's travelling the same road."

That said, I knew a small pathway that not many people ever took, on the right-hand side before you came as far as the crossroads; you could've passed it before you even noticed it, tapering away as half-hidden between two ditches overgrown with rocks and stones. It passed by Slowworm's Mire and through Fugitive's Wood, past Drowned Dog's Pool and over as far as Manslaughter Hollow. Whoever passes this way suddenly arrives at a thatched house as half-swallowed up by the ground and set against a tall craggy rock choked up with bushes and briars. It was here that I was born and reared, and here too was where my mother was born, in addition to both my uncles.

On returning home, my mission complete, my young head was always spinning with controversial issues and questions.

"Uncle Maurice! We all have to travel the same road from now on," says Uncle Philip. He says that there's no point going against the tide of life. The stream flows to the big river and every river to the great sea just as all roads lead to Dublin… and from Dublin to London and Tokyo and Los Angeles… and…to all the other great cities. People everywhere have to leave the countryside and make for the cities. That's what Uncle Philip says! And he should know!

Chapter 10

" Aye, aye, aye. Your Uncle Philip would know all right! Maurice would respond sarcastically. "And God knows, we were tired listening to the same old blather out of him!"

"The streams flow out to join the sea! Where the ocean plankton lives (he didn't tell you this bit, did he!) all of it piled up on top of the rest, the same as the people who live in the big cities... aye! Like the people in Dublin and Tokyo and New York, all packed in together like ocean plankton. And didn't I bring you to see the salmon leaping against the weir? And didn't I explain to you before how the ancient Irish always had a great respect for the salmon's knowledge and nobility? And you don't have to be like all the other people, all crowded and squashed in on top of one another in the city! You can be as clever and as knowledgeable and brave as the salmon and set your nose against the current of the times so that you replenish the shallow pool that gave you life in your first days." Says my grandmother then:

"There's a shower of rain coming over the brow of the hill. You'd be as well off taking in your Sunday shirt from the hedge outside."

Says I:

"But wasn't it out of the sea that every living creature came in the beginning Uncle Maurice?"

"It was! Various life-forms escaped from the overly-competitive parts onto the land millions of years ago. In much the same way, other living creatures escaped high into the sky by developing special wings to help them fly a few million years later again."

"Well, there you go! The brave man never lost it!" says my grandmother, a woman that wouldn't be silenced for too long no matter what the subject of discussion.

"Not you've ever shown much inclination for flying yourself come Sunday when you've a damp shirt stuck to your back!"

"Little Packie," says my Uncle Maurice, shaking the creases out of his damp shirt with gusto.

"It appears that the entire world is going is on the wrong path. We need to return again somehow to the path that is reasonable, Christian and wise."

Chapter 11

Having thought about this for a while, says I: "Granny! Uncle Philip says that the parish priest is losing it!"

"You shouldn't say the likes of that about the priest—even if it's true," she says. "I don't know what Father Fury ever did on him anyway?"

"He says they'd be better off closing down the old school instead of keeping in it open anymore! He says we've enough problems without bringing in a German woman to run it. He says most of the Main Road people want to send their kids to the County School."

"I can't see what's wrong with having a German woman as a school teacher?" says Maurice. But he spotted Granny staring at him curiously. In response, he says in a challenging tone. "What's the harm having a new face to look at amongst the local women?"

"I don't know myself," says Granny, "what he has against the old school where he learned everything he knows about mathematics and making money anyway."

"Ha!" says Maurice. "I heard that the County Council are planning on widening the road but it won't be happen until the old school is demolished and cleared out of the way. I heard that this'll change the layout of the roads so that double the traffic will have to pass our Philip's garage and shop straight away."

"According to my Uncle Philip," I pipes up, "the population of the parish is falling from year to year and it won't be long before all of the houses in the parish are all the one type—the exact same as the ones on the Main Road."

"Maybe so," says my Granny. "Out on the Main Road, the houses are all numbered and accounted for. And the same with the people living in them—the same as clerks in government offices. This means that it's easy to keep them all handy and close-at-hand and to keep everything under control—between their names, addresses, ages, jobs—and every other fact and information about them. Isn't it always easier for them to manage and control the information in these cards and files than it is to control the people whom the information refers to? Isn't it very easy for them to gather all their files together so that the government clerks can mess around with them whenever they feel like it?"

Chapter 12

Needless to say, I had no intention of telling my Uncle Maurice everything that my Uncle Philip had told me. Uncle Maurice would have gone ballistic and he'd have been ranting and raging for the rest of the night—so I kept the various things that I heard down in "Valleymore Services" to myself.

"There are some people," says Uncle Philip, "and they can never be controlled or organized properly until they're arranged in a box on the day they're put into the ground, God help us! The same as two people who're close to you and me Packie! I've no patience whatsoever with people who're always trying to keep make life go backwards! They're only fooling themselves! When the whole world is moving in the one direction, the person who sets themselves against this thrown to the side or trampled underfoot. All you've to do is to see that the houses are skirting the road these days. Most of the people living in these houses have cars even if the odd elderly person amongst them that still takes the bus. Everyone travels by road one way or another these days. When we were young, we travelled across the fields. On a visit to someone. Or to buy something from the shop. Now, that's no longer the case however. Everyone goes by road now. If something can't be got in the post office next to the church, it's to the big towns that people go to buy it these days—to the big supermarkets. And anything the supermarkets don't have—it's to Dublin they go to get it. East East East is where the roads lead, eastwards to Dublin, that's just the way things are!

"What's the point in complaining though? You might as well give out about the stream that flows into the sea? What else would it do? There's a crowd out there who'd prefer to see the river flowing backwards against the hill. There's no answer to what's happening now. The way things are going, with the constant improvement of the roads, and transport service, it's important to make help the living stream of people travelling to Dublin move more quickly—and afterwards onto all the other capital cities abroad. According to the statistics, the number of people living here is declining from year to year."

This was Uncle Philip's take on it all but I couldn't let him out with all of it—no more than I could let him tear the house apart. There was an old German war poster high up above the hearth that my Uncle Maurice brought home from his travels on the ships abroad; it was white and blue and had the word "DEUTSCHLAND" stamped at the bottom of it. It was a print of s soldier dressed in the uniform and helmet of ancient Rome, sword in hand and holding a shield.

"Is it one of them—a German woman like—who's coming to teach us in the National School soon?" I says.

"It is, I suppose," says my Uncle Philip, "except that she won't be wearing the uniform or be armed."

"Uncle Maurice! Didn't you fight against Britain for the Irish cause?"

"I did."

"And my father fought for England against Germany?"

"He did."

"But why?"

"We were afraid that the Germans would take over England and there'd be no sense in that whatsoever. Because it's in the prophecy that the Irish have to do this."

My granny interrupted them:

"It's fated that we Irish Gaels will one day drive the entire spawn of Westminster into Hell and trap them inside the filthy hole they came out of with a giant rock!" "God help us," says I to myself. "God help me and my two uncles and my granny! And the children in the old school! And this woman teacher coming over to us from foreign parts! And she as clueless about things in County Leitrim as I am about algebra!

Chapter 13

Up here in Dublin, where I live these days, people don't understand how to hold an interesting meeting.

They don't even think that meetings should be interesting! There is total confusion about these matters. Hasn't it been long-recognized by our Gaelic ancestors that there's no point in relying solely on talk and speech to solve the problems of the world. All of the ancient Gaelic concepts have been lost to city people however and all they want is talk, talk, talk and more discussion still. What they don't realize is that talk doesn't achieve anything that throwing a few punches and threats around wouldn't. Now, I'm not saying that we didn't have a few debates and discussions in our Parish Hall. But at the meetings my two uncles attended, the discussion was generally seen as a prelude to prompt action. The pacifists are right to say that trouble and strife emerges from a lack of understanding between people. This wasn't how we saw things however. Familiarity breeds contempt and argument. And it's unusual to fight without also offering terms of peace as the old proverb goes. As regards my two uncles, peace terms were always necessary before battle could truly commence. At Sunday Mass, the day that Father Fury announced he'd chosen a woman of Germanic descent as our new teacher for the old school, he felt a murmur run through the congregation like a shuddering wave and he knew that he'd split God's people right down the middle.

"A meeting will be held in the parish hall to discuss the question of the new schoolmistress," he announced. So that nothing could hinder all the parents attending, he said that small children would be allowed to attend the meeting also. (This is how there were enough younger people present at this historic meeting to ensure a reasonably trustworthy account of what was said there, one that is on the record to this very day...)

Father Fury initiated proceedings as follows:

"At this point," he says, "there's no harm in me mentioning something about the woman this discussion concerns. Now, even if she is German, she has full Irish citizenship in a manner of speaking because she was born and reared here. She's the daughter of man who was one of the German engineers that came to this country as part of the Shannon Scheme in 1928. Her father ensured that she educated herself well in both cultures and traditions. She got some of her training in Wales and some in Germany and she completed her education by studying Celtic Studies at the University of Aberystwyth.

My Uncle Philip barely listened to any of this as he'd already decided what he was going to say on his way to the meeting. And there was no reason for him to waste his well-prepared words, was there?"

"For the love of God," he says. "In a civilized Christian, Catholic country like Ireland here—that our own parish priest would open the door to the barbaric teachings of Nazism!" And, of course, this gave Uncle Maurice the opportunity to add his own tuppence-ha'pennyworth to the proceedings. How could the Nazis have been so bad if they were fighting against the British?"

Says Philip then:

"Give this 'Irma Grese' of a schoolmistress—as imported to us from the country of the death camps – just a few weeks our innocent little angels here will be doing the goosestep and wearing the same-coloured shirts and bawling out—*Sieg Heil! Sieg Heil! Seig Heil!*" This statement of his was dramatic and powerful in equal measure and it elicited a loud roar of approval and a big clap from the listeners who weren't on Main Road Philip's side at all. This didn't derail Father Fury however and he ploughed on with the meeting regardless:

"It is clear to me that there are some people in the parish who are very unhappy with the woman I've chosen as our new teacher... And I will admit that others have been recommended for this job instead of her..."

"It is my responsibility to carefully weigh up the various applicants' qualifications however. And I duly did so before deciding that there was no-one else amongst them as well-qualified as this woman of noble European heritage whom I've chosen, the Baroness von Cheep, to give her her correct title."

But the objectors weren't happy with this and felt it necessary to push back against it.

"Don't we have a qualified teacher in the parish already?" someone asked. "Don't we have the Publican's Son? And he already fully-trained by the Christian Brothers."

"It is true that the young man you mention received a certain degree of training from the Brothers," says the priest, "but as far as I know, the Publican's Son is on the run from them at the moment. I'm just an ordinary parish priest, you should understand... and there's no way I could steal one of their recruits from a group as disciplined and well-organized as the Christian Brothers and emerge unscathed from the encounter. What I would recommend is that you pray for the chick that fell from that particular nest...that God may grant him the courage to surrender himself up to them again. For fear that organization's anger fell on us..."

Said my Uncle Philip:

"Wouldn't we be better off considering a woman whom we all know well, a learned woman full of knowledge and facts. I'm thinking of the former postmistress Nora Feathers? She'd make an excellent teacher when it comes to disciplining the children."

"She'd be good without a doubt and I'd have been quite happy to appoint a woman like her to the job… if only her eyesight was as good as it used to be," Father Fury responded.

A supporter of Phillip's was next to speak.

"Now, what about one of the older local gentry from this area here? Someone who's always been very fond of children… I'm thinking of that elderly and very-dignified warrior, a person who likes nothing better than the company of youngsters… Colonel Moustache."

Father Fury hesitated momentarily before responding:

"It's true that the same man is living back here in the parish again."

"I didn't know he'd ever been away. The young kids must have missed him. Was he on holidays? He told us that he had a sailing boat over there on the Mediterranean…"

"It's said that he came through every war without so much as a scratch," another woman said. "And he still as tall and straight as a whip. And he really does love children, as you said yourself, love. Was he on holidays so Father?"

The priest chose his words carefully. "On holidays? You could say that. He was, in a way, I suppose. He wasn't on a sailing boat however. He was actually sent to hospital, to tell you the truth. He was er, er… a patient… in the mental hospital."

"Tell the truth straight out Father," my Uncle Maurice said. "He was damn lucky that he didn't go to jail and that fondness for children of his was the reason for it too! The dirty old yoke! He should've been neutered years ago!"

Chapter 14

"You'll see," the parish priest said, as soon as things had calmed down a little "why I'm so happy with the woman I've chosen for you. We are incredibly lucky to have the likes of her available to take up the mantle in the old school. And I am also absolutely delighted to say that, despite her Germanic background, she has an incredible interest in our nation's ancient music and she is also fluent in our native language."

Irish and music were wonderful things my Uncle Philip piped up, but in such a sarcastic way that you knew by him, he'd rather have seen the seven-headed, ten-horned monster rising out of the sea than either of them really. But my Uncle Maurice really went for him straight away then, even if everyone within hearing range of him did their damnedest to ignore him:

"Music? Wouldn't it be great for the children to be able to play music? That way they'd be able to play a few tunes on the streets of Dublin someday and they'd be able to get by while looking for a job there, wouldn't they? Likewise, the Irish language would prove very useful to them when they emigrated in London... so as to get a job in construction—seeing as most of the work is divvied out the between Donegal crowd and the Connemara people."

This was my Uncle Maurice's take on the whole issue. My Uncle Philip countered by saying that some of the parents from the Main Road would prefer to send their children by bus to the fine new school that had recently been built in town. The County School as it was then known.

"But the old school never had a bad name, had it?" the priest asked.

"The Main Road parents wouldn't like to find fault with the man who's gone…" said my Uncle Philip

"Too good for their kids it was, and that's the truth," Uncle Maurice retorted, but Uncle Philip just shrugged his shoulders and tried a different tack.

"The Main Road parents want a teacher for their children who can expand their overall life experience, so that they have better opportunities once they leave school."

"So's to turn them into a bunch of little stuck-up snotty noses, is it?" said my Uncle Maurice.

"They don't see music and Irish as the two best subjects for their children to make contacts socially with business people and future employers, that's all," Philip added.

"You mean, when they've no choice but to leave and sell themselves to the highest bidder at the hiring fair, is it?" Maurice batted back at him, and there was a collective intake of breath as the priest gave Uncle Maurice a filthy look.

A murmur of anger rose up from Phillip's followers, one of whom shouted out:

"Come on Father! One of our own women teaching our children. That's all we're asking for here."

"Aye," said Morris, "one who's as pig-ignorant as the rest of you!"

"Now, that was going too far. It was nearly enough to really kick things off?" Everyone's eyes shifted over and back from Maurice to Philip and from Philip to Maurice again.

"And they say that this woman who's half-German has opinions too." another female supporter of Philip's stated.

"Opinions?" cried the priest who'd never been too quick on the uptake.

"That's right. Opinions of her own."

"Of her own?" the priest repeated with a look of surprise.

"Yes. At a meeting in the County Hotel. She was heard saying that ordinary people can develop their psychological and mystical powers and elevate or enhance themselves both mentally and physically."

"But isn't that the true objective of education really?" said the priest.

"Father, they say that the German woman believes in Liberation," the same woman added.

"Liberation?" Father Fury said, with a look of confusion. "Women's Liberation," the woman who was with the Main Road group confirmed, a hint of impatience in her voice. "I didn't want to have to say it with the children listening and all…"

"Huh!" the priest said loudly. "I think that all the women in Germany are like that."

And you could see him thinking for a second:

"If you've nothing worse than that against her…" he said. Philip made one final attempt however:

"But Father, is it wise to have a foreign woman—about whom we know nothing—teaching our children just so's to keep the old school going? When we could send them all off on a fine modern, comfortable bus to a fine, modern, comfortable school and make them into fine, comfortable, civilized citizens."

"To make them into drawing-room dolls more like," Maurice spat back and this was the final straw. Both men stared one another down and it was as if an ancestral war spirit had come down from the sky and lit the ferocious battle-torch within them. They immediately turned their backs on one other and walked away in opposite directions to the edges of the crowd, one man turning right and the other left. Circling the gathering, both men faced off again and then before anyone had a chance to come between them, the brothers did battle with their blackthorn sticks—until the priest put a stop to the spectacle.

All told, it had proved a wonderful, exciting public meeting!

Chapter 15

Women's Rights? What about Schoolchildren's Rights? And when will the Girl's Army declare war on the life and culture of the Grown-Up Faction?

And aren't we, as schoolchildren, the perfect revolutionary class according to how Karl Marx viewed the world? The group whose only hope lies in the day of battle and their numerical superiority on the battlefield. Children have another trait that will stand to them come the day they declare war on the older generation and this is the excellence of their intelligence services and their ability to gather information. Because children are usually ahead of their parents and elders when it comes to the seeds of every new initiative in society.

The older people get, the more cynical they get about modern life. After a while, they they'd prefer if everything went back to exactly the way it was before. Or if something is different today from how it was yesterday, they'd rather not know about it at all.

Soon, even the news no longer seems new and everything that happened today follows the same pattern as yesterday. This is when the old crowd feel they've triumphed over the younger generation. That's where they're deluded however because once they lose their curiosity for life, they've chosen to live in ignorance from then on. From this point onwards, they're only letting on that what they call knowledge is in fact a form of ignorance.

A good example of what I mean here was the dispute at that meeting concerning the new schoolmistress. If all of the Main Road group had known everything about the German woman that was already common knowledge amongst the local children, they'd have had the information and propaganda at their disposal to turn Father Fury against her far more quickly.

The priest thought very highly of her because she loved the Irish language so much. What he didn't know was that she believed strongly in the Irish fairies also. We children knew that she had views and ideas that were fairly unusual though. She believed that ordinary people could enhance their natural powers and abilities greatly and that they could raise themselves physically off the ground by willpower! She was already experimenting with such techniques personally herself and we children had definitive proof of all of this. Between Irish language and music, and all the rest of it, Baroness von Doze was well-qualified for her new teaching job. It is true that she hadn't a great understanding of how the educational system in Ireland worked. But this gave us children the opportunity to shape and adapt this system in more imaginative ways as suited ourselves; we were even able to create new branches of Irish education that hadn't been heard of prior to this.

This German was the sort of woman who was quite happy with her own concepts of education and educational systems and she paid no heed to the curriculum other than to see how we could make it her own. She was one of those people who'd rather have been dead than live in a way that was lacking in the artistic. And if she hadn't been able to develop school-teaching into an art form all its own, she would have resigned. If one considers teaching to be an art form in itself, then it is important that every teacher have their own concepts and philosophy of teaching—just as every artist has their own philosophy of

39

art. But there is at least one other major difference between the teaching art and every other art form. The painter or sculptor can spout their theories and views to the rest of the world but the teacher has to remember that he or she is working in a living, shifting, medium. The walls of the studio will not betray the painter's secrets but children have ears. Worse still, they also have little legs beneath them so that they can run home and carry all of these grand, new words and concepts back to the grown-ups. And this was how things began to unravel for the Baroness; this is where she first went off-course.

And wasn't this exactly how things were ruined for many intelligent people before her? The people who over-think matters and make a mistake are often the ones whose lives are turned upside-down. Replacing action with over-thinking is like putting the cart before the horse. Talking about how something needs doing rather than just going ahead and doing it when it needs to be done.

Chapter 16

By rights, the Baroness should just have forged ahead and kept her plans to herself. She should never have mentioned any of her objectives and theories in the presence of the children. She might have got away with it then. It was a mistake on her part to explain her educational theories to a class full of children. She'd have been way better off just teaching away without ever revealing all of the underlying theory and unusual ideas that accompanied it. The children brought this information home with them—or at least—what that they understood of it anyway. The housewives took the children's words and created something even more interesting out of them.

The men got anxious about it and went down to the pub to get advice from the others. The trouble was only beginning however. It didn't matter so much that she taught the children terms such as *gestalt*, a word that they translated as "Gestapo" down in the pub. It wasn't a huge issue either when it went around the area that she used a teaching method developed by Mussolini. It was easy to get words like *Mussolini* and *Montessori* confused after all! But the word that did the all the damage was *Bauhaus*. Even nowadays, amongst Irish people who are fairly-educated, it's not everyone who can tell you much about the German *Bauhaus* movement, a group who had new and radical theories about art and education. To tell you the truth, we knew very little about the German language or people around our place back then.

The education we had when I was growing up was based mainly on a handful of elderly people scattered around the local area who spoke the purest of Irish as passed down to them from the seven generations before them. On hearing this foreign term *Bauhaus* for the first time, one of the older people decided that this unusual word was a very dangerous one, as relating to sorcery and the most sinister aspects of the "black arts." The word *Bauhaus* put someone in mind of the term *Buarach bhaithise* in Irish, a term used in sorcery that means a piece of dead person's skin.

But all *Bauhaus* means in German is "building house" or "working house". The Bauhaus Movement that thrived in Germany at one time—its fame and renown spread far and wide. In the early days, students who came to learn this new art form from them were usually asked to sit at a table in an empty room—a table on which various bits and pieces of rubbish and odds and ends were left—a squashed can, a piece of timber or an empty bottle for example. The apprentice was asked to create something new and artistic from these various cast-offs.

At this point, dear readers, I recommend that you source a reliable account of the history of the Bauhaus in Germany and read it carefully.

Chapter 17

As it turned out, the new teaching system Baroness von Doze implemented with the children of the old school was actually a slight adaptation on the basic theories of the Bauhaus group. She would gather together a small collection of materials- small bits and pieces that might have appeared useless on a first glance—a stone, a screw, a hook, a nail, a button, a hazelnut, an empty jar, a scrubbing brush, an empty box, a piece of coal, a bottle top.

She had her own reference scheme set up for each of these items so that she could record the reactions and responses of various children to her teaching methods on different dates, and to analyse them and compare them with one another. (The Baroness was German to the core and similar to Germans everywhere, she had a high regard for exactness and accuracy. She had all of the children's names listed next to a special code in addition to the dates of each trial or test and the various items and materials utilized. She also had a big heavy master-file or ledger that served as a reference key and ensured the results of the entire project were more comprehensible. In addition to this book, she used a number of smaller notebooks to organize and plan activities from one day to the next and a series of very large white posters hung from the walls all of which recorded the results of various tests and trials in very fine detail. As I say, she was a German to the marrow of her bones.

At this point in the story, dear readers, it is important to introduce you to little Anna, a small, weak, half-blonde girl from the school, who was always lacking in energy. Anna had very pale features and big grey-blue eyes and she had the look of someone who was wandering around in a dream from morning to night.

Over time, as the testing programme of Baroness von Doze took effect, a number of small, strange incidents began to happen around the school. At first, some of the materials that the children had worked on during the day went missing from the school cupboard where they'd been carefully put away. Every morning, the Baroness noticed that one or two items were missing from where they'd been left the previous day. The items in question would be discovered again fairly-quickly but always in a different place from where they were left previously. For example, they might be lying on the floor somewhere, on her desk, or on the windowsill. This situation continued so that items were being shifted or moved around at least three or four times a week. Unsurprisingly, the Baroness began to suspect that some individual or group was breaking into the school after it'd been locked up for the night and was moving things around for some strange reason.

The best thing a woman as scrupulous or organized as the Baroness could have done at this point was speak to the man whom she held in high regard from the very beginning of her tenure there, the parish priest, Father Fury. People don't always choose what is best for them in every situation however, do they? Even highly-organized and conscientious women, like the Baroness. In addition, as it turns out, she had good reason not to call into the priest to discuss this matter in the end.

Chapter 18

Given the long tenure of this world's ancient enemy deep down in the bowels of hell below, it seems that some of the finest people in this world just can't get on with one another. Unfortunately, this is exactly what happened in the case of our very able and dutiful schoolmistress and our most honest and sincere Parish Priest and it was an awful pity how things turned out in the end. Because no one was more taken with the Baroness in the beginning than was Father Fury. He was completely enchanted by her initially and if it hadn't been for the strictures and obligations of his high office, I'd say he probably would've fallen in love with her. He could have used his love of music and the Irish and German languages to plead his case, couldn't he? But wait till I tell you now how it was that their friendship cooled and ended over time.

Father Fury was a kind and understanding priest but as with any good man, there were one or two things in life he just couldn't stand, things he'd never have had any time for—even if he'd lived to be 300 years of age.

Amongst these was the mentality that many Irish people refer to as "the poor mouth" syndrome. Father Fury understood what real poverty meant and consequently, he was always the soul of generosity whenever he found himself amongst the poor of this world. As regards the sad bunch who used poverty a weapon however—he had no time for them at all—they drove him mad altogether.

As mentioned earlier, he had enormous respect for Baroness von Doze—this was until one day he spotted her rooting around between the dustbins on the edge of town. Quietly, he saw her take a bashed and dirty-looking tin can out of a bin and take it away with her as happy as it was the most valuable artefact in the National Gallery. Father Fury put this to the back of his mind however until one day when he was on a school visit and found the Baroness in the middle of the class and all of her pupils focused on a similarly ugly bit of rubbish. The priest left again without so much as a word; he was so upset that he clean forgot why he had called to the school in the first place. He was disgusted that this woman whom he'd assumed had the highest respect for everything dignified and cultural was using rubbish while teaching the children of the parish! He just couldn't believe it! And he wasn't going to put up with it either! Father Fury would have happily toured all of Ireland if she'd asked him to find a beautiful book for the children. He had friends in America who'd have sent him on the very latest electronic, educational devices available on the market if he'd asked them to! He'd have raided Maynooth on the children's behalf if there was no other option; he'd have gone as far as the Vatican for them. And yet the Baroness preferred teaching the children with rusty nails, stones from the side of the road, bits of dirty coal and empty jars. He couldn't understand all this stuff about "Bauhaus" and he just got more and more angry with every attempt she made to explain her strange theories. Father Fury just couldn't see any benefit whatsoever with poverty or hardship or want. Ireland was a country with a long history of poverty but thankfully, this era was gone. It was true that the Germans had suffered the devastation of the two world wars—one after another. Things had been very tough in Germany for a while but this couldn't explain how she was teaching the children. Using filthy pieces of coal and empty bottles! There was no need for that! Was this woman completely crazy?

The Baroness didn't call on the parish priest however and he didn't call on her either and this only exacerbated the lack of understanding between them.

As you can see now, dear readers, this woman was in trouble. Just as the Allied forces had pushed in on the Third Reich in 1945, this brave woman's difficulties were closing in on her from all sides in 1957. We can't explore all of these issues at this juncture of our story or it will prove a tangle of confusion however. We'll explore them one by one instead.

Chapter 19

So here—we find our female hero sitting alone in the school-house as night draws in. She has sent the children home hours earlier. A single lamp streamed onto her a table where she had all of the various recycled items required for the children's work carefully laid out. The Baroness herself was examining her copybooks and ledgers with the various trials and test results noted in them. This was something she did almost every night of the week. On this particular night, she was working later than usual and she'd no intention of returning home too early either. A thought had struck her that day which had sent her hurriedly poring over her files carefully again.

Suddenly, as if in a flash, she realized exactly what she was searching for in these various files and why she'd been keeping them all along—even if she'd have liked to have been mistaken about it. She stopped momentarily and raised her head from her copybook, pen poised between her fingers. She had no particular reason for abruptly adjourning her work, just an intimation of something. The sound of the wind getting louder outside perhaps? She got to her feet and glanced over at the table where the various small objects were laid out in orderly fashion. She focused her eyes on one particular object…

Suddenly that object moved! There was no doubt about it! A big empty jar. Shining and clear on the bright on the dark surface of the table. Like a pawn shifting position on a chessboard.

And then it shifted again—at a 90 degree angle this time. She sat back into her chair and murmured to herself.

"If it moves a third time, I'll go mad. And if it doesn't move a third time, I'll go clean mad too. Maybe I've gone stir-crazy already!"

The Baroness knew right in that instant that she had the proof that her perusal of the files would have confirmed. But she decided to complete her scrutiny of the books anyway— even if she already knew exactly what it would confirm.

Earlier that day, hadn't she asked one of the girls to focus her mind and thoughts on that same empty jar and to share the outcomes of her meditation with the class the next morning? Little Anna was the girl! Now, the Baroness knew it was her that was behind this whole business. Whether one could have referred to this phenomenon as the work of a poltergeist or not—this was a whole other question.

Chapter 20

That there was the teacher's perspective on events. Hers was only one side of the story however.

Has any government report ever been as accurate or as detailed as that of the ordinary man or woman in the street? It hasn't and it never will be either and this is the truth. All the big words and fine talk on the part of the establishment and the state and they spouting their own take on history and its affairs to all and sundry. If every historian was to be entirely honest however, they would say that it's the people who stood ragged and barefoot on the cobbles and the streets who truly understood this game. That it is the mob who understand the real truth of things—if it was only possible to get it out of them?

It goes without saying that it wasn't easy for our new schoolmistress to prioritize my role in the running of old school or to acknowledge it even—this despite the fact that I had no difficulty whatsoever in recognizing her role and responsibilities. Children understand the necessity for patience and tolerance in such matters in order to remain in tune with the rough, irrational and arbitrary nature of the adult world. But there was more to it than this in my case. Seen through the Baroness' eyes, I was about as significant as the keys of a battered, old piano. Have pity for me, why don't you? Sure, I was barely ten years of age yet! Worse still, I'd fallen in love with her—something that didn't make my life any easier, I can assure you! I barely registered on her radar and no wonder too! She didn't want her authority in the school undermined in any way. I could tell that any attempts at compromise with her as regards influence and standing within the school were a non-runner. So, for the sake of the peace, I decided to learn from her when she spoke on a subject that I understood a bit about—international history, for example.

In the meantime, our interactions in the scholarly sphere where fairly fraught—with her doing her damnedest to teach me things and me trying my best to protect my soul from education.

That said, I would give in quite easily when it came to the history lessons, as this was a subject I could link with aspects of the world around me—the perennial between both my uncles, the irrationality and craziness of my granny—and my own experience regarding the abilities and otherwise of those in authority and power.

Back then, I saw National School as a reflection of the state in a manner of speaking. The teachers were the leaders of state, the spokespeople, even if their power was quite dependent on keeping the parents sweet—the latter were the faction who kept the teachers in power after all. The children were the people who had the various rules and regulations forced upon them and they alone understood what was going on and how the system operated in reality—if they'd only had a way to make this information public. They were the fodder for trial and experimentation, the same as the lobster who's flung into the boiling water on the stove—all they could do was give the odd screech out of them; they were powerless to do anything else! If the Baroness was perturbed by the fact that some of the small materials used in her trials and experiments were appearing and disappearing as if they had lives of their own—imagine what a young girl of nine years of age must have been thinking now that she found herself wrestling with internal forces that seemed beyond her understanding and control!

Chapter 21

If Little Anna was worried that adults might find out what was going on in her case, she was even more determined that the other children in the school didn't—albeit that it wasn't that easy to hide things from them.

In fact, even before our schoolmistress had understood the problem for herself—before she even knew that there was a problem at all, in fact—the other schoolchildren had worked out Little Anna's secret—the secret of this small girl's paranormal abilities. This actually proved a great source of relief to Anna.

That which had been a great source of anxiety to her prior to this now proved a source of fascination to others—and this was a huge relief to the poor girl—even if they were still just children like herself. And she was even happier 6again when she saw that the other kids were neither frightened nor horrified at her secret power either—but actually jealous instead! That said, it wasn't long before various skittish types who knew her well were asking Little Anna to demonstrate her skills for the most ridiculous reasons and just for the fun of it.

Given that, even as a youngster, I understood the responsibilities that accompany power of various types, I considered it my duty to protect Little Anna from all of the crazy and ridiculous requests she received. It wasn't long before the day came around that the adults realized what was going on however.

THE MIGHTY WOMAN'S ADVENTURES ABROAD

The Main Road crowd who'd never liked the Baroness in the first place now had the evidence they needed to show the priest what sort of an individual he had put in charge of the old school! Poor Father Fury, he was horrified! Was this the reason for the various items of rubbish she'd collected? That they were magical or paranormal items of some description after all? That he had set up a school of witchcraft or the paranormal in his own parish under the auspices of this crazy pan-German, pan-Celtic druidess from the heartlands of Europe. What would the bishop say? And the poor children he had led astray! If he didn't deserve excommunication for this, it was only just about!

These thoughts were probably going through Father Fury's mind the day he arrived into us at school to give us a long lecture about the Cathars, a group that had caused the church a good deal of concern during the tenth century by all accounts. They believed that this movement belonged to the world of the devil. And even if the Cathars had been wiped out as a group, the priest said, it was still incredible how many people lent credence to beliefs of this type. I agreed with Father Fury about this immediately. Because it seemed to me that—even if I'd never heard tell of the Cathars prior to that class—I was one of them myself. If what Uncle Philip said was true, then the whole world was travelling in the one direction. And according to the people whom I held dearest—my granny, my Uncle Maurice and now this schoolmistress from Germany—this was the way of the devil. Even if I didn't like Philip's views on the world, I still knew only too well that he was the only relative of mine who'd any chance whatsoever of making a few quid in times to come. And the way I saw it—the one thing most people tended to ignore only very rarely in this world was the issue of money.

Father Fury himself, I says, peering at him carefully with the sceptical eyes of youth—he was someone else who was always looking for money, naturally enough. And the devil was unlikely to give him any money given that the priest was on the wrong side, as far as he was concerned, the priest would've had no choice but to ask people who were on the devil's team for some money. And given that the devil owned the entire world, it was highly unlikely that he—above anyone else— would be willing to help the parish priest keep things running in the parish!

The world was in an awful state because the devil had the upper hand in most things—real love was always left in the halfpenny place and an absence of love was always in the ascendant. Love was like a beautiful plant growing by the way-side. Next thing, indifference and a lack of care comes along like a massive digger that destroys the plant and tears up the ditch and half of the field—after which a load of tarmacadam and concrete is poured over it. Even the biggest fool in the world could recognize the treachery that lay behind all of this. The one chick that was your pet amongst the garden chick-ens—that was always the easiest one to catch and kill for the cooking pot.

A kingdom or sanctuary of this world as governed by the rule of love!—how incredible such a place would be, if only it existed? Even if its reign and sovereignty would without doubt have proved quite a short one.

Chapter 22

There is nothing that annoys adults more quickly than when their own children prove their equal. Often, you'd be forgiven for thinking that they didn't want to admit that they belonged to the same species as their children even. It is always a major source of disappointment to such people when they see their own sly and sneaky ways reflected in their progeny. And as for the same snobbery or arrogance! They go into a rage when they see their own anger and ferocity reflected in their children. They feel ashamed when their own greed reveals themselves in them and it frightens them to witness their own lack of scruple reflected in them—and the tendency towards dishonesty and deception.

I'm not denying that there is a small group amongst them—the adults that is—who recognize the truth even if they have nothing to hold over the younger generation other than the extra time they've spent polishing their skills in the aforementioned arts and acquiring more experience in the finer points of the game. Let no one ever underestimate the years spent by the older generation garnering valuable knowledge about every activity and game on the face of this earth either. And the older generation should be forgiven too for the angry rants they let out of them every time they remember how much of their precious time they've wasted senselessly in years gone by.

Any clever child will always give members of the older generation the same advice as they would their parents—not to waste their latter years on stupid, boring or dead-end activities—but rather to live life as fully and vibrantly as possible—so that they are equal to the next generation of livewire children springing up around them like nettles in the raspberry bush.

Because of the unusual status I had gained in the school back then, I had many dealings with grown-ups. For this reason also, children often came to me seeking advice about their relatives and it was the same issue that bothered them most of them—i.e. the adults telling them lies! And I always gave the children the same advice in every case—to take things easy and to give the liar plenty of rope to hang themselves. It is only natural for the child who discovers that older people haven't due regard for the truth to be upset about it. There is always the danger that on recognizing this, the child in question reacts too abruptly or hastily however. This is the why—in case one has to pay later on for a sudden impulse—that it is far better for the child to adopt a relaxed approach with the elderly deceiver or cheat and feed them as much rope as they require. It is important for children to remember that it is never easy for the older generation to change tack or amend their ways; this is why the liars and frauds amongst them maintain their dishonest and deceitful ways—at least for another while.

Yes indeed, the rashest response of the lot therefore is to contradict or confront the liar immediately. By doing so, the falsity or lie is not completely destroyed and the elderly chancer or fraud is only bolstered in their belief that they can deceive the youngster and still get away with it. One should never destroy this possibility completely therefore, and the best policy of the lot is to happily go along with their deceptions so that the lies get bigger and more outlandish from one day to the next. As with a giant sea rock or an iceberg, it is better for a lie to be a big one—so that you can see it coming from miles away! The best strategy of the lot then is to encourage the fib-teller and liar when they are in full-flow and the more embellished and exaggerated the yarns they spin.

Eventually, the day comes around when their statements become so ridiculous and outlandish that even the youngest and most innocent child in the country wouldn't believe a word of them. The liar finds themselves isolated and alone out in the middle of the ocean of their own exaggeration and stupidity. So much so, that their pet dog would barely pay take any notice of them!

Whether the liar or windbag deserves their punishment is of little importance; what matters is that people are protected from the lies and false information.

On the other hand, if the older crowd is forced to change or better their ways against their will, they may become cuter and more careful in the future with all the lies they spin. Consequently, you're always better off not to cast too much doubt on their tall stories; otherwise, they'll put far more preparation into them beforehand to ensure that they have a more credible ending.

Chapter 23

I may have been the Emperor-King or *Generalissimo* of all the children in the village but at the end of the day, I was still just a child. And in my heart within, I still had great time for the German schoolmistress and huge respect for her. Not that this did me much good however, seeing as she considered me a rebel and an instigator of trouble and anarchy at all times. Given this misunderstanding regarding my status and standing in the school, she saw me as the fly in the ointment from day one. I couldn't see any way of resolving this conundrum—and unfortunately when things came to the crunch—what did I do but only let her down?

That day when her job in the school was teetering on the edge, I found myself in a terrible quandary. I was torn in two inside. I was like a tiny boat trapped in the inlet's choppy waters, trapped as I was between the wild river-waters and the raging sea—that was the day that I really suffered, I can tell you!

This foreign woman who was our schoolmistress had generated nothing but jealousy and hatred from her first day in the job—until they fired her for a finish. And as for the Main Road crowd, they provoked me and incited me against her any chance they could. And they encouraged the other children to incite me against her also. Adults would stop me on the street and urge me on to greater efforts. There was me—stopping with my Uncle Philip at the time and trying to make a few shillings working in the garage—with the same seditious and goading talk in my ears day in and day out! And yet, when all was said and done—I gave in to them in the end and let her down.

I had great respect for the schoolmistress but she didn't understand what I was going through at all; she hadn't a clue. But isn't that how things often are in this world?

I enjoyed the company of my Uncle Maurice and I liked his ideas on freedom, but when push came to shove and my granny needed money to pay the bills—it was my Uncle Philip that she had to rely on.

That said, I hated Philip's narrow and black-and-white outlook on the world even if I understood why he'd such little respect for people who lived the dreamland of old stories and heroes of days' past. The way I saw it back then was—everything in life was political at the end of the day. The devil had power and control over everything in this life and the majority of people were in his corner. For as long as children never had the vote, it was highly unlikely that the forces of love would ever triumph!

My Uncle Philip had promised to arrange lodgings for me in Dublin and to tide me over with a little money until I managed to find a job there after finishing school. In my heart inside, I still hated Philip's view that the whole of life and the world was going in the one direction. That said, we all had to live life as it actually was—and not as we'd like to have found it.

What else could I do but bow down to Philip and give into him however? The fact that I was still just a child then was my justification for the fact that these adults dictated to me what to do—the crowd that wanted to run the German woman out of town. Then again, I gave the order on the morning of that fateful day when all the children walked out of school. The majority of the kids didn't want any hand or part in it but ultimately, it was a question of discipline. I'll never forget the look of surprise in her eyes as she watched us walk out and then the anger that overcame her afterwards. She didn't know that my heart felt dark as coal in that moment and that I felt really terrible at the role I'd taken in the whole affair. The Baroness gave up teaching shortly afterwards. She also left her home in the south of the county and moved away to Dublin.

Woe to he who does evil and who finds themselves poor. Needless to say, Father Fury wouldn't agree to the old school being closed or knocked down. He saw it operating there for few more years yet. As for myself, I'd switched sides when it came to my uncles. Uncle Maurice couldn't forgive me for siding with the "Main Road Faction" as he always called them, by going against the woman from Germany. And even if the old school did go on for another while, there was no widening of the road there and no further expansion of "VALLEYWORE SERVICES" either. If he'd built an extension to it, Uncle Philip wouldn't have had any few pounds left to support me while I was in Dublin.

The publican's son, the man who'd been on the run from the Christian Brothers, returned home and Father Fury appointed him teacher instead of the German woman (a poor substitute if ever there was one). I myself put in another year and a half at school while ignoring the new teacher completely, and dreaming of the person who'd been there before his arrival. To give him his due, he never bothered me at all one way or the other. He just avoided me the same as the cat skips around the rain-puddle. I was no longer the leader I'd once been. Not that there was anyone else who was qualified to take up the mantle; the role remained temporarily unfilled. I was still held in some respect around the local area but it wasn't the same anymore. Other children may have made way for me when I walked by but they didn't make a beeline for me, awaiting instructions as before. That era was over. And I preferred it this way too.

Chapter 24

On finishing school, I found myself in the same boat as most youngsters of that generation in Ireland—trying to make sense of the world and relate the reality of life as I found it to my understanding of it from the day I'd been born. I attempted to do all of this in a way whereby I also managed to make a living and trying to fit in with the various people I came across.

I spent a while doing bits and pieces of work in various cities across England, then a while at the same crack in Ireland—with stints at home in Leitrim and in Dublin. And I won't deny that I struggled more in Dublin than I did anywhere else. As regards the Baroness von Doze, our clash on the battlefield of education had proved a short one. But had I won the war? One thing is certain—she turned her back on education after that.

The local parents also did their damnedest to try and ensure that she didn't have a chance to say goodbye to us also. And even if Father Fury was busy locking the door and the school gate as he accompanied the Baroness on her last day in the school—a gang of us decided to make a sudden incursion over the wall and surrounded her in a big group right between the back of the school and the toilets. Father Fury didn't do anything to try and prevent us. Instead, he stood stock-still nearby, his face twisted in a strange combination of horror and amazement as he listened to a fierce and passionate speech from her, a powerful oration that put the hair standing on our heads and that engrained her image forever in the minds of everyone who heard her. The stunning image of a beautiful warrior-goddess who was as strong and powerful as Krupp steel itself! As she said in her speech on the last day, teaching methods were being employed worldwide, the objective of which was to destroy the natural spark and energy of youth.

On arrival in Dublin, I wasn't long hearing the many stories that were already doing the rounds concerning the Baroness. Dublin people are very proud of the fact that strange or eccentric people from foreign parts live there and settle amongst them. In pubs, I heard tell of this wealthy female druid from Germany and her experiments in levitation.

A mythology was already developing and spreading amongst the many Dublin idlers about that house on the south-side of the city where one could get a mighty feed of German food— and all just by hinting to this extraordinary woman that you believed in the mystical world of fairies, levitation and gliding on the air.

Not that she was a soft touch by any means. There was no fear that anyone would take advantage of her. Any man who tried wasn't long finding out found that this woman wasn't going to be pushed around by anyone. And if this didn't do the job—she had two male bodyguards with her at all times—one Irish and one German. They were both as different from one another as day is from night, because where the German was odd and tempestuous in his ways, the Irishman was as polite and relaxed a man as you ever met. Also, the Irishman was always well-suited and booted whereas the German wore odd-looking hats and cloaks and all sorts of strange rig-outs. It wasn't as if he needed to attract attention to himself anyway seeing as he was 6 1/2 foot tall and enormous in size; in contrast, the Irishman was small and light. And that wasn't where the contrasts between them ended either. The Irishman was known simply as "Socialist Sorley" but the German's surname was nearly as exotic and strange as the man himself. Would you credit it? His surname was only a form of intimidation! I am Erfurt von Volcaniceruption. Herr von Volcaniceruption to the likes of yourselves. And the thing I hate the most is when people can't pronounce my surname properly. Hey—you there man! What's my name?

Next thing, he'd go on about how easy it was to break some-one's bones! But the most incredible thing of all about this bizarre trio—the Baroness, von Volcaniceruption and "Social-ist Sorley"—was that they spoke Irish to one another most of the time. As for me, the more I heard about them, the more curious I became about everything to do with the Baroness von Doze. I lapped up all of these stories about her and took every-thing in, then did my best to separate the truth from the fiction. I tried to distinguish the person I knew from the character described in all of these stories based on exaggeration, half-truths and invention.

Part 2

Chapter 1

I was twenty years of age and getting by one way or another in Dublin city. Pulling the devil by the tail behind me to make ends meet and moving from one temporary lodgings to another, always searching for the best chance of finding casual work. I got to know people here and there who'd give you a meal or stand you a pint if you were stuck—on condition that you didn't go begging them too often. I wasn't living the life of Riley, that's for sure. The life of the hungry, healthy, scavenger dog more like!

Some of you reading this are too young to know what life was like in Dublin around the year 1957. I'm not sure how I can give you a flavour of the era! You crowd with your giant-screen colour televisions! What's the point in me recalling those days now when you could buy a hen's egg for a penny and a duck's egg for cheaper than that again. You tall, gangly teenagers today with your navy-blue jeans! Ask your poor tormented mother how much bread and butter costs, and add in tea, sugar and milk on top of that—in today's money. Well I know that my mam would bring home all of these in her shopping bag back then and it wouldn't have set her back more than three or four shillings. If she happened to call into the butcher shop after that, she would have got a pound's weight of sausages for an extra eighteen pence! Excuse the teary cheek and the sad quiver in my voice when I recall the lovely sausages of that era!

(There are many people nowadays who don't eat meat at all, myself included! And would you blame them either?) Because nothing in this life is how it once used to be. Even the cattle of the fields don't get treated fairly. But I'm thinking back now to the days when if you wanted to, you could have had a fine meal in any café on O'Connell Street for just three shillings! A half-crown for the same down in one of the cafés by the docks in the morning.

But wait till I tell you about the pints back then too! They were so thick and creamy and so nourishing that you'd have to swallow them down quickly for fear they swallowed you instead! Back then, the pints went down in a way that made you feel they might take a big bite out of you if you didn't sink them in the one massive swallow. It was...

But where are you all heading off to? Or is it that you don't believe me? The young people of today! You can't tell them anything!

Chapter 2

Gradually, I began to find my feet and settle into life in the city. Not that this diminished my curiosity regarding a certain woman! A woman who'd left her mark on me as a very shy schoolboy. I could have gone directly to her and thrown myself prostrate at her feet. I could have done but I didn't. Instead, I got to know the man who was friendly with her—or at least that's what they said anyway. "Sorley Socialist" was called "Sorley Socialist" because he was a socialist. They said that he'd read Engels and Marks and Lenin. Freedom of speech, he'd say, is the greatest freedom that any nation seeking to expand the education of their citizens requires.

The mentality which Sorley outlined here was typical of the type of Irish people back then, I think—a curious mindset open to new ideas and ways of thinking. It was a different mindset as compared with that found amongst people today—and this despite censorship being in place. I don't plan on trying to explain this to you now. I don't really understand it fully myself! In a strange sort of way however, a certain freedom of speech existed then that doesn't exist now and this is how there were so many interesting views and philosophies doing the rounds at the time. All I can say is that there was a special feeling of freedom in the air between the years 1957 and 1958 and in following years. What surprises me most now thinking back on that era is the number of people you met then who had great plans for the future. People who had original and definitive schemes laid out in order to solve all of our many national problems. When I think back now on how certain these people were regarding the efficacy of their strategies and plans and how angry they'd get if you doubted them in any way, it always amazed me how few of their plans and schemes ever came to fruition and how many of those concerns and problems we still have today. Indeed, many of the same problems were not sorted out since! Unless the changes were imposed from the outside, that is. And certain issues and problems have actually got worse in the meantime, believe it or not!

There is no question however but that there was an atmosphere of freedom and idealism in the air at this time. There is no doubt whatsoever about this. You couldn't fling a stone across St. Stephen's Green without hitting a philosopher or theologian of some class or other. (The Catholic theologian with the papal encyclicals on the tip of his tongue, the Protestant theologian with his Bible under his oxter and the Marxist theologian who was rarely beaten in an argument. Any stone that didn't strike a philosopher of some description it would have bounced off a language scholar instead.

Well, it would've hit an English-speaker at the very least, someone who'd have chatted to you for a quarter-of-an hour without drawing breath on the subject of how to save the Irish language or (alternatively) how to wipe it from the face of the earth forever. Either that, or the stone would have struck someone who'd have explained to you for a quarter-of-an-hour why it was a waste of time to debate the language question at all.

Aye! There was a freedom of speech back then undoubtedly. Particularly for fools! But maybe that isn't a big change at all.

I'll tell you now how I first got to know "Socialist Sorley" the first day ever.

Chapter 3

Many city pubs used to be half-empty back then. I went into pubs one day with barely the price of a pint on me. I was young at heart however and always hopeful that my luck might be in—and had a keen eye for anyone I might be able to bum a pint off. There was only one punter in the pub already however and I could tell by the barman that he was at the end of his tether trying to keep this fellow happy. And this punter didn't have the look of a tourist about him either. Or that was in a better way money-wise either! Was he a betting man I wonder? Maybe. But this man's talk was all politics and not horses! The customer went off to the toilet and, the publican turned to me and said between gritted teeth:

"He's a Socialist!"

Stranger still! I actually knew this barman from years earlier. The "Cold War" was going on at the time and he was very interested in everything that appeared in the newspapers about it. Back then, he was really worried that Ireland might turn Communist and that his pub would be confiscated from him— and that he'd be sent home to the family farm in Leitrim and have to work it communal-style. Well, I was all ears now anyway as he told me the story, all nod and wink. I nearly fell off my stool that second however because two big, heavy men came bursting in through the door. They were just two detectives who'd arrived in for a quick chat—something to do with court cases down in Green Street or some

sorry prisoner who was banged-up in the Bridewell. Not that I thought this on first glance. In fact, for a second or two, I imagined they might be two members of the Soviet Secret Service who'd berthed their submarine under the Halfpenny Bridge or down near Aston Quay somewhere. Our Socialist friend returned from the toilet right then and it was back to the real world and the main topic of discussion again! The revolution in Ireland was just around the corner was your man's theme—and it was easy to prove this also, he argued. Because the capitalist system in Ireland was already on the way out—ever since they'd raised prices and made a bottle of Guinness a full shilling exactly! A shilling for a pint of Guinness! Things were gone absolutely crazy; the capitalist system had spun out of control completely. Who could deny it in all honesty? The working-class would revolt any day soon and there was no contradicting the Socialist on it!

Even the barman himself couldn't argue much against that one! Because even a blind donkey could see that the world was falling apart.

It was sometime around then that the air transportation people made a major breakthrough and smashed the sound barrier. An aeroplane could fly faster than the speed of its own sound for the first time ever! Not that this news bothered the people of Dublin much at this juncture. It was difficult enough for them to believe the increase in the price of a pint—never mind that it might ever break the two-shilling "sound barrier" at some point. Well. That's how life was back then—around the time that I first got to know Socialism Sam or Sorley the Socialist for the first time.

Chapter 4

Despite the personal hatred this publican had for Marxism in his heart inside, anytime a Marxist put his money on the counter to buy drink, he made a point of listening politely to every word that came out of his mouth. I myself wasn't much more scrupulous in this regard either. We were all Catholics and knew that Marxism was the antithesis of this but then again, neither *Quadragesimo Anno* nor *Rerum Novarum* had laid down any specific church teaching with regard to drinking pints in Marxist company. There was a lack of specific direction as to how the faithful ought to deal with such situations. The protocol I followed in doubtful cases like this where the necessity for political discussion arose—it made no odds whether it was Socialism or Georgism that was in question—was that I could be as political as *Dáil Éireann* (the Irish Parliament) as long as the drink kept flowing. I suppose you probably think that I listened to Sorley hoping that he'd stand me a pint? Well, he did! And not only the one, but he stood me the second pint and a third pint also. And if he didn't stand me a fourth, I'm certainly not complaining. It is never a wise move to be tight when it comes to buying pints but one shouldn't go over the top either. It is better to remain measured and balanced in all aspects. It is fine for someone to be a Socialist as long as you don't get carried away with the whole thing. One pint is enough to be polite and a second one just to be friendly;

if the third pint was poured for the Socialist cause, the fourth was just plain fanaticism. The barman had no problem doling out porter to a Socialist and I had no problem drinking it either. Other than that, the most he got out of us was an occasional nod or murmur of solidarity. When it came to the revolution, the economic realities were a major impediment to the publican.

The way I saw it, I was in the same trap as him; whereas he was too rich to side with the revolution, I was too poor.

Because the concept of the welfare state was still just in its infancy then. And given that I only had occasional employment or work without stamps or insurance cards, I figured that I wasn't able to take an active role in the international revolution on the side of the working class. If I'd had steady work, I could've called a strike against my employer but, then again, I had no job. And if I'd been in receipt of the government's unemployment benefit down at Denmark Street along with everyone else, I could've raised the revolutionary flag and joined in the huge protest marches of the unemployed.

It was Napoleon Bonaparte said that an army marches on its belly. In that case, the army of the unemployed usually marched in a very unmilitary fashion. Napoleon wouldn't have been impressed in the slightest with how they organized themselves the best day ever. And the ranks of the same army that weren't entitled to any welfare had an even more decrepit and worse look about again. Rather than marching on their belly, they were crawling along the ground more like. They were a right disordered-looking crowd when it came to battle. No doubt about it, they marched to an uncertain beat, they were all over the shop really.

But choice accompanies ambition—so that the man who has a job is in a stronger position than the man without one. And the man who's unemployed yet receiving unemployment benefit is always in a stronger position than the man who doesn't get any welfare at all. Those in the third category who've neither a job nor the benefit of social welfare are the lost foot-soldiers of the revolution, the people who are lost in no-mans-land...the *status quo* has appeared wind-side of them and scattered them a long way from the main ranks of the workers' army.

This would have been far too complex an issue to go into with this Sorley fellow whom everyone referred to as the Mister Socialist. And I had good reason to be thankful to him too. Hadn't he got me to understand the reality and circumstances of my life more clearly?

I left the pub, my eyes scanning the length of the Liffey, the Quays and O'Connell Bridge and a thought struck me. If the capitalists were oppressing the workers so strongly, as was claimed, wouldn't it be far better to side with the capitalists?

Chapter 5

Well—I'd got to know the man who was quite friendly with the woman who'd inspired me when I was young -and he was a socialist. He was clearly approachable and open-minded in his ways... and keen on influencing others to try and improve this society of ours. (Rather than making things worse which is what most of us try and do!) A major improvement in my case would have been a renewed friendship with the woman I'd secretly looked up to and adored as a youngster. This was a very different thing from politics and political discussions however. This might have been me reaching beyond myself.

Reflecting on this in silence, I said goodbye and left the pub in a disconsolate mood, as indifferent to Socialist Sorley's Socialist teachings as I was on arrival.

It wasn't society and the human condition that was bothering me now however but rather the Socialist's relationship with the German woman. I couldn't have cared less about his views on public issues as compared with this particular aspect of his private life! My curiosity about this pair was tormenting me. Not that there was any malice in it at all; it was just a budding curiosity on my part at this point—as a tiny new plant sprouting from the earth in early-Spring. If it was let grow unhindered, she'd possibly have changed into something else entirely—something very prying, Iago-like, jealous, desirous, arrogant, malicious and destructive. But at this stage, there wasn't the slightest harm in it.

I was still just a young buck then. It was true that I'd met the Baroness before Sorley had ever come across her. If I'd been the jealous type, wouldn't I have been well within my rights being jealous about the whole thing—if I'd been that type, that is...

As I found out over time however, it wasn't difficult to get Sorley onto the Baroness as a topic of conversation.

"She might be of German stock, but she's a Gael all the same," he says one day.

"They say that she's a druidess," I says.

"They shouldn't say that about her," says Sorley.

"But don't they often say that she tries to fly up into the air" I says.

"What it involves and what she believes possible aren't the same thing as flying however. There is a report of a member of the ancient noble Albanian family, the Home family, who managed to raise themselves off the ground, all of them in an straight line, before witnesses—in and out of a window on the third floor of a tall building. Levitation in this way is possible but the most effective techniques for this still need further work and development. We are increasing our knowledge on the rules relating to this phenomenon from day to day. There was a man in London during the final years of the 19th century who announced that he would be raising himself from the ground on a certain day out on Hampstead Heath. The police claimed that he would be breaking the city council's rules regarding the governance of public parks and that his plans were illegal. They tried their best to stop him but the man managed to fool them and performed a public demonstration in front of a crowd of people despite them.

"I never heard that story before."

"Maybe you didn't but there was a full account of it in the *Times* of London and I could show to you if you like."

Sorley continued but I was no longer listening to him. It was difficult for me to believe that I was walking the along the street with someone who was in regular contact with the woman I'd love to have had walking next to me—more than anyone else in the world. I'd a right to be jealous of Sorley seeing as I'd fallen in love with this woman before I was even tall enough to reach up as far as her waist. If I'd been the jealous type, then I'd have been well within my rights…

Because I'd known that very attractive and fine woman well a long time before Socialist Sorley ever laid eyes on her. People know others or think they know them. This man who liked her thought he knew her, but in truth, he hardly knew her at all.

I knew the Baroness in a way that Sorley never would. I knew things about her that he wouldn't have known even if he was married to her. I knew things about that woman that she didn't know herself. Oh, if I'd been a jealous person, I had plenty of reason to be jealous!

Chapter 6

"*Dear Sorley, you don't really know this woman at all, not the way I do. I know her as well as the child whose eyes are fixed on their National School teacher all day long and hanging on their every word. Maybe you've sat next to her drinking tea once or twice and exchanged a few opinions with her but I sat beside her and keenly absorbed every word she said during my younger years when everything I learned was fresh and new. Every word and thought of hers is inscribed and filed away in the computer of my mind. I could play them all for you now no problem if you wanted to hear them. Maybe Sorley you have gone so far as to look into her eyes or take her hand in yours? But I gazed on her for six hours a day, five days a week. And I did so with the great wonder-filled eyes of childhood that are entranced by all things! I know every aspect and trait of hers. Wasn't it from her that I learned whatever small morsels of knowledge that are in me? She was my teacher Sorley and she'll be a part of me forever. If she'd been a film actress Sorley, I'd have seen her every film a thousand times! People say that the love of a young 10-year old boy for a grown woman is nothing compared to that which binds an adult man and woman. They say that a 10-year old child has little understanding of a woman's beauty and that there's something unnatural for a child of that age to be in love with their teacher. But they can say whatever they like, who cares? She might have left me bewildered and con-*

fused sometimes at school and yet she was always steady and consistent in her manner towards me and treated me with nothing but indifference and contempt. And now, after all these years, it seems likely to me that she has changed little."

"What's wrong with you?" says Sorley suddenly. "You're not listening to me at all? I'm wasting my breath talking to you and you not paying the slightest attention to me." He was right of course. I was lost in my own thoughts but quickly snapped out of it.

"I was thinking Sorley. You know that stuff you mentioned earlier—that thing about yourself and the Baroness von Wink and the levitation—it's like something that you'd read about in the old biographies of the saints long ago. But who takes any notice of the likes of that anymore?"

And Sorley just continued with this bizarre and crazy stuff, explaining it all to me again.

"Y'know that it wasn't from Irish folklore or reports in English newspapers that the Baroness first got the idea for levitation—but from a religious sect that we no longer hear much about—because they were run out of their homeland by the Bolsheviks in the 1930s. The Hope to Heaven group they were known as and the most interesting thing about them, as compared with other groups, was the emphasis they put on CO-OPERATION and mutual assistance within the group. A special sense of understanding was required between the members of this group any time they found themselves in danger or under threat in some way—or whenever they undertook a particular activity or task. It was part of their history—that a group of their predecessors were surrounded by the their enemies on one occasion, enemies who were intent on wiping them out—but, based on their solidarity and hope in one another—they'd found a way a way out of their predicament and escaped by levitating into the air and disappearing. Their enemies had looked on in amazement as the entire group had flown over their heads and escaped their deadly clutches. From that time on, as part of their religious ceremonies and rituals, they always tried to capture that same high point of empathy and union that had helped their ancestors escape mortal danger years earlier. Sorley went on and explained that their interest in levitation wasn't the whole story as regards this sect from southern Russia but also their belief that a group of people with a common purpose could focus their minds in unison thereby achieving what might seem impossible initially in human terms. And it was this aspect that first attracted the Baroness' interest in them:

"She says that every race, group and people in the world have a myth of one kind or another that keeps them strong and that gives them courage in the face of life's great trials and difficulties. A tradition and mythology as held in common is what emboldens an armed group in war-time. A mutually-shared myth is also what puts the *Sword of Light* into the hands of the ordinary people and ensures they are heroic in the face of their people's enemies; any group of people can achieve that elevated point of hope and trust in one another to ensure that collectively, they can achieve anything in this life.

"It is this philosophy of mutual solidarity and effort that the Baroness has adopted so that she believes it is still possible to save the Irish language from extinction.

And this is the task that she has set before herself—to organize and enable such an important communal effort and initiative amongst the Irish speakers of Dublin city. If she succeeds in leading a small group of these Irish-language enthusiasts and activists in line with such a united communal philosophy and initiative for—say a year and a half—she will have achieved something incredible in itself. It would prove more powerful an achievement than twenty newly-formed Irish language movements or seventeen state strategies for saving the language ever could."

"I see," I said, insincerely because I didn't understand a word of what he was on about; and I didn't believe a word of what I could understand of it either. I was thinking of something that my Uncle Philip used to say:

"People who believe that the Irish language can be revived would believe in anything! And it struck me then that if they if what they sought was a united group of people with a common aim and purpose such as this, they'd have found it far easier to unite them against this initiative than they would have for it.

Chapter 7

As mentioned earlier, there was an amazing energy and vitality coursing through Dublin city back then. I got to know incredible people and incredible things happened to me also. And it was in the Irish language community that one came across the strangest and most incredible people of all. It was a far cry from nowadyas where everyone is bonded together by the fact that they all have the same opinions and views on everything.

And in the pages that follow here I'll tell you about some of the most bizarre and remarkable of the Gaels that I got to know during this period. The likes of Brendan O'Worried and Talking Wolf, the Foreign Professor, Erfurt the German Irish-speaking giant von Volcaniceruption each and every one of them as odd and as amazing in their own unique remarkable way. Having said all that, I knew deep down too that the Baroness wouldn't have had the time of day for anyone who wasn't fluent in the Irish language.

Now, on an initial glance, you wouldn't have thought that there was anything particularly remarkable or incredible about Socialist Sorley—not unless it was how incredibly normal he was...

But once you analysed the situation more deeply, you found that he was the most incredible person of the lot really. His incredible relationship with the incredible Baroness was

incredible in itself. After all, it was incredible that he could promulgate socialism while at the same time palling up with this
upper-class Baroness from Hitler's own country. And as for
Socialism? What sort of socialism would her type have
espoused? Astrological or paranormal Socialism? And the pair
of them as puffed-up and as self-important in themselves as
you've ever met in your life!

But then, if you looked at the Baroness and the group she
gathered around her, and the way they became obsessed with
Irish at the same time that everyone else in the country
couldn't care less about the language, this too was quite incredible also.

And one of the main attributes of the Irish language that
makes it exceptional or incredible from every other language,
is that the people with the best knowledge of the language don't
consider it worth the effort speaking it. I said to myself that I'd
have to find someone who was very serious about the Irish language—so I went to one of the highest officers in the Irish language movement to seek advice. Having listened to me carefully at first, he paced up and down the floor of his office. Then
the chief officer gave his opinion:

"The person who's most deeply-tormented about the fate of
the Irish language today is that sensitive and gracious soul that
is Brendan O'Worried. Here's his phone number." He wrote
down his number on a card and then pushed me out the door
of his office again. Brendan O'Worried is the type of person
who's very sensitive—not sensitive on his own behalf however
but on behalf of others. "A Bleeding Heart!" He's the type of
person who'd give socks and shoes to the ducks out in the field,
if he was let do so. He had Irish. He was very worried about
Irish. His own Irish. And the Irish of others. Would the Irish
language survive? Would it die out? Whatever her fate, he was
worried about it.

Another source of anxiety to him was that some people became too obsessed with Irish and they suffered as a consequence. Ah... the Irish language!—many's the decent scholar's mind that it got the better of and destroyed. I know of scholars who came here from abroad when Irish was still spoken in every county in Ireland and they went completely over-the-top with it. Some of them fell head over heels in love with the Irish language. There's no harm at all in a bit of "Más é do thoil é" (Please) or "Go raibh maith agat" (Thank you). And a bit of "Conas atá tú?" (How are you?) or "Gabhaim pardún" (Excuse me) never hurt anyone. But there's a crowd out there who get carried away seeking out the names of every different type of animal and plant, people who record and register every little detail—total fanatics. It's rare for any Irish person to let the Irish language get such a grip on their mind and their senses. But it's well past time for us to do something about these poor foreigners who learned too much Irish through ignorance and misunderstanding. I've never lost hope that one day we'll have a government that faces up to the crisis of the Irish language head-on. They should open health clinics in every parish for people who've overdosed on Irish, therapy centres for everyone who absorbed too much of the language before realizing its dangers.

Chapter 8

It wasn't enough for Sorley to recommend that I learn Irish but he also had to bring me to all the different venues and occasions which the Irish-language crowd frequented, so that I could become more fluent in the spoken language. He even brought me to a big Irish-language event where I got to meet the most incredible of all the people in the movement—Dr Don'tmindit.

A small man, you could tell from his bearing and clothes that he wasn't from Ireland originally and two large men accompanied him everywhere for his protection. It was certainly difficult not to take notice of him.

"Hey Sorley, what in God's name does that buck do for a living?" I says. "Or who is he?"

What immediately sparked my curiosity was how reluctant Sorley was to give me a straight answer however. He, who was normally quite open about responding to questions, it was obvious that he was reluctant to tell me anything about this low-sized and mysterious little man and his minders.

"That man's business has nothing to do with the likes of us, thanks be to God," Sorley says. It's unlikely that you'll have any dealings at all with him. Not unless you have to call on the services he offers to a certain class of Irish people, that is."

"Is he some sort of doctor then?" I says, with a guess.

"He's a sort of a doctor alright."

The most expensive doctor in the country by all accounts. A doctor of Psychology, he calls himself. Dr Don'tmindit. But let's not discuss him any further for the time being. It was clear that Sorley hated this man so much that he preferred not to hear his name mentioned at all—whatever the reason!

The strangest thing of all was that how mistaken Sorley proved with regarding to the doctor and I. Because I got to know Dr Don'tmindit very well and had many dealings with him before this story was done.

Next, Sorley recounted the story of the Baroness' first body-guard Erfurt von Volcaniceruption.

"He has a very hostile attitude towards the world, doesn't' he?" I says.

I said. "There's a psychological problem at the root of that," Sorley says. "As a child, Hitler took power and von Volcaniceruption was made a loyal member of the Hitler Youth. It is difficult for people today to understand how taken the younger generation were with Hitler and his movement. Back then, it was unimaginable to these youngsters that they could be beaten in the war and when this happened, it weighed very heavily on their minds. Many people just couldn't cope and broke down, and some committed suicide. To see Hitler defeated was as devastating to them as the sun falling from the sky. And when a body of people experience a shock as enormous as this, each individual seeks their own personal resolution to the issue. In Erfurt von Volcaniceruption's mind, with Hitler now dead, a woman had taken his place—the Baroness von Doze. There was nothing she asked him that he didn't do for her...immediately. She sang the praises of the Irish language to him and he became fluent in the language within a year of his arrival in Ireland. It was here in Ireland that he found what he'd been searching for—for so long—the meaning as to why Hitler lost the war between 1939 and 1945. He heard that a small number of Irish patriots had sided with Germany in that same war. And this was enough of an explanation for him. Because von Volcaniceruption had already researched Irish Nationalism while learning the Irish language. Based on this, he'd come up with his own theory on these matters. It was because he'd had a few Irish supporters that Hitler had lost the war!

You can see now dear readers how wearisome it was for me to have to listen to Sorley endlessly praising to the skies this woman whom I already knew a good deal about. One day, I decided to put a halt to his gallop on this score and exact a bit of revenge in the process. He was banging on with what was by then a well-worn tune of his—how this German woman had such a deep interest in Ireland and Irish culture—when I suddenly put a halt to his gallop!

"If memory serves me rightly she didn't have much respect for Irish people though, did she?"

"What do you mean!" says Sorley, with a horrified look and I was ready for him—my answer on the tip of my tongue.

Because at the end of the day, a child's mind is like a sponge or a tape recorder. And if schoolteachers understood this, they'd be far more wary of opening their mouths in front of a class full of children. Especially those teachers whom children might consider a bit unusual or exotic—a German woman, teaching in an Irish National School for example. A woman whose every thought and utterance was indelibly imprinted on my mind. I couldn't have forgotten her words even if I'd wanted to. Poor Sorley! I think he thought some evil spirit from the depths of hell had just taken possession of me. If you'd seen the look of horror and fear he gave me then—as he listened to his cherished Baroness' exact voice and words emerging straight from my mouth. It was all he could do to stop himself from punching me!

"Before visiting Wales my favourite thing in the world was the ensemble singing in unison that the Germans love. But in Wales

such ensemble and group singing is taught to children at school. As a consequence, everywhere you go, you come across the Welsh singing together—in the pub or the church or at the rugby match—they are all singing in natural harmony together. It doesn't matter what type of song or music it is—whether it's a hymn or an international pop song or one of their own native Welsh songs. They have an appropriate harmony ready for it. On arrival in Ireland, which is referred to as the Country of Music!—I found the exact opposite to be the case however!

Where the Welsh sing for their own enjoyment, the Irish sing to frighten their enemies and the art lies in trying to drown out the voice of the person next to them and subdue them. The women trying to out-screech each other with their sharp wailing—the same with the men roaring and bellowing loudly—so as to deafen the man next to them. Whoever can't emerge victorious with roaring and bellowing from the depth of their lungs does a strange brassy bellowing of his own that is difficult to ignore.

All of this is indicative of the fact that individualism and competition is deep-rooted in Gaelic culture. Cú Chulainn took a lone stand at the ford: and if there is comradeship in the stories of the Fianna, the same tales are replete with single combat also. And as regards singing, it is every Irish person's dream to achieve renown as an unaccompanied singer! It annoys the Irish singer usually if they have to raise their voices in song at any everyday event in the company of their fellow-Irish—if they sense that others wants to take part in the song. The singer deem it insulting to them that someone else would seek to take part or that they'd be challenged—and there is a certain logic to this. Because there's nothing worse in the world than two or three Irish people singing unaccompanied simultaneously. On the rare occasion that the Irish have to sing together, it is out of a deep hatred for something that they are all the united against that they do so. This is clear from the terrible caterwauling they make when singing religious *or political songs. To give the Irish their due, it is as a war strategy that one should assess their singing. It is an anti-peace technique on the same level as the war dance of the Zeybeks in Turkey. As with Turkey, Ireland isn't a country for people who have no fight in them. He who stands his ground when a group of ordinary Gaels are singing together demonstrates enormous fortitude and courage."*

Chapter 9

The day eventually the day came around when I received an invitation to visit the big house out in Kilmacud in order to take part in some of the unusual experiments being conducted by this strange group of half-Irish/half-Germans. And even if I was happy to go there with Sorley now that I was getting to know—or re-acquainting myself—with this amazing woman and her followers, I could tell immediately that I would be partaking experiments that lacked any logical basis. I didn't go there for the purposes of reason in other words but rather for the purpose of the irrational. On my way out there that day, I fully understood that it was magic and craziness that awaited me and that I'd be surrounded by complete incomprehension and confusion.

Now, I'd heard about a saints of the church—Saint Joseph of Cupertino, who'd levitate into the air regularly with joy and happiness.

What got me was how a man who'd always been associated with Socialism could have gone in this direction in the first place at all! I'd never heard that Karl Marx had levitated through the power of inspiration while writing *Das Kapital*. Or that Lenin or Stalin had been into levitation a whole lot either. If everything we heard about them were true they'd sooner have blown anyone who didn't agree them away with a grenade or a rocket than glide up into the air themselves! And if Sorley was a true Socialist why the sudden fondness for this Baroness, a member of the upper class from Hitler's country? Had I only got half of this story really?

"Yourself now Sorley—seriously—do you really believe in this floating in the air business that she's promoting?

He got a bit angry at this.

"That there now is the sort of thing that would make the Baroness doubt you straight away. Can you not see that we are trying our best to inspire hope and confidence in people here? And there's you then with the same old cynical attitude as always, despite everything! People who believe in miracles is what we're looking for But sure, you don't even believe that the moon is in the sky above! The most important part of our project is to ensure that everyone remains focused, body and soul, on the one united objective. And all it takes is one cynic to destroy all our efforts. There's another thing you should know. This woman is a German despite her commitment and dedication to the Irish language, she has little patience for the lackadaisical attitudes of the Irish. Or with the "ah sure, it'll do grand" attitude rather than just getting the job done properly. I felt a partially-disguised threat in the last bit of what Sorley said there. At the time, though, I didn't see this as a major cause for worry.

Chapter 10

A long-standing and traditional aspect of the Irish-Language Movement over the years has been the organization of dances and céilís. So, Sorley decided to organize a series of céilís. He organized the band and got the tickets printed and it was Baroness von Wink prepared the sandwiches, I had no doubt about the objective behind these dances. What else could it be except to make money for some secret fund in support of the Society for Levitation? A scheme to generate finances for some dark campaign as planned from the big house in south County Dublin! However, when this céilí proved a disaster they decided to organize another, and then another one again. They say that the Russian Ballet wouldn't exist today it hadn't been for the unlimited power the Russian landlords held a few hundred years ago to demand whatever they wanted from their serfs. Some of the people who organized céilís had an attitude similar to the upper-class of old Russia, so much so that you'd have thought they were possibly descended from them. You'd never have thought by them that they knew 20th century people had rights and were free to attend whichever events they preferred—or stay at home if they preferred to do so also! However, the way the organizers of Gaelic occasions acted in those days, it was as if all they had to do was announce the fun-filled upcoming event and all the serfs would come running! (Sometimes they even forgot to announce the event and yet still expected a crowd to show up!) Sure, what else would Ivan have for doing but combing his beard and changing into his Sunday best? Pull out the high shoes that his grandfather got married in, give them a polish and get ready for the Grand Céilí. I'd have thought that the likes of Sorley would've had more sense than this but maybe the fault wasn't his and maybe it was the Baroness herself who'd got it wrong. Whatever the case, it took them a while to get the hang of how to organize céilís properly. And as with learners everywhere, they learned the wrong way initially, and the right way only later. As for me, all I learned during this period was how to live off stale sandwiches because I always had a big box of them with me going home from every unsuccessful céilí. It's incredible how quickly the human spirit tires of the same food. Sandwiches with jam or some other kind of sauce or seasoning in them—they just don't taste the same after a week. Some of them turn in on themselves and close tight and others flop open and turn all stinky. A fortnight after you've made them and even the dog would turn them down. That said, the Liffey seagulls are always hungry and they're rarely fussy about what food is on offer. I have a theory—even if I can never prove it—that the Baroness was hoping these sandwiches might lead to my death. But they didn't.

Chapter 11

As outlined earlier, organizing céilís has always been an essential historical aspect of the Irish language movement. The céilí that proves a failure is rarely mentioned afterwards however. One couldn't write the history of shipping without many references to shipwrecks and losses at sea, for example. But when it comes to the annals of the céilí, the ones that proved disastrous are never recalled or recounted. I witnessed a few Great Céilís that sank completely. I remember the occasional social disaster—from which the only people who emerged unscathed were the one doorman, a pair of fiddlers and the odd member of the organizing committee. There's nothing as terrible in this world as a social occasion that proves a disaster. If the public doesn't show up, there's nothing be done except turn off the dancehall lights and lock the place up again. And rarely does it prove that simple either! More often than not, the organizers have to negotiate tactfully with everyone seeking payment—the musicians, for example. As soon as they've fixed up with the musicians, the custom is to carefully gather up whatever money is left over from the entrance receipts in the hope that there's enough left to stand the cost of a *postmortem* in the nearest pub. When things are really bad is when one has to fall back on the help of others, it goes without saying, and it's a bad state of affairs if there aren't one or two loyal supporters of the cause knocking around to buy a drink for the organizing committee of this latest disaster. Then it is time to focus once more on the bizarre and inexplicable mentality of the ordinary people of Ireland. It is this mysterious factor that is denoted by the letters *TSLCNSU*—The Shameful Letdown of the Crowd that Never Showed Up. It is also then probably that the realization hits home—i.e. that there's more to organizing a céilí than simply hiring a band and booking a hall. Settling up honourably with the parties involved is the most crucial aspect of all to sort out. It is not unreasonable that the band go home with the prearranged payment as agreed beforehand, even if they haven't played a single note of music. They're entitled to this because they've fulfilled their side of the bargain—being present on that date and prepared to play music, even if they've only the empty walls as a sounding board. *Fair play* is all that anyone can ask for. And anyway—how can anyone who avoids their responsibilities and refuses to pay the piper—how can they ever hold their head up high again in any company of Irish people? The mortal shame of it! They'd hardly be classed as Irish anymore and they'd have been better off leaving the country altogether.

My new arrangement with Sorley, for as long as it lasted, was based on the precept that Sorley recognized my attitude of dissent—i.e. that I would do any number of favours for someone who didn't push it too far and tried to push me around. After all, young people crave their freedom at the same time as they like direction from others. And to make sure that Sorley never spoke to me as if he was ordering me around, I kept a closer eye on him than I did on anyone else. He knew that I'd travel the whole of Ireland on my backside naked rather than doing anything that I didn't want to do. It goes without saying therefore that I assumed responsibility not for the music on these occasions, but rather for the non-music.

That awful racket that came from one particular musical group who would never see payment! And this was a far from pleasant task! I've a few stories about that, I can tell you!

We normally referred to the time between 9 and 10 o'clock at night as the "time of reckoning" for the céilís as it was around then that we knew whether any bit of a crowd was going to turn up or not. This was the critical hour for which the dance was remembered one way or the other—as either the "Great Night Out" or the "Great Fiasco!" Sorley always got very nervous around this time and he'd have me tormented trying to make sure that the crowd inside already didn't change their minds and decide on leaving again. One of his strategies to keep things ticking over was for a handful of our supporters to arrive in the hall in flying form, hang up their coats and move in relaxed fashion to the back of the hall at which point they promptly skipped out the back door again. Then, having swapped coats around outside the front, they'd magically come back in through the front door again, supposedly to pay their way in again a second time.

This, Sorley claimed, made it look like a big crowd was streaming into the hall. This plan of his never worked as it required a level of organization that the Irish-language could never muster!

Slowly but surely, the céilís began to prove more successful. Not that Sorley still didn't get stressed about them sometimes and that he didn't try and pass on some of that stress to me also. It wasn't enough for someone to come to the céilí once if they didn't come back again another night. This left him worried about the "wallflowers," the girls who weren't ever asked out for onto the dancefloor. Sitting next to me, Sorley would spend the evening singing the praises of these women and prompting me to take them out for a dance. Over time, consequently, I became very good at forcing conversation on them and getting them chatting, and discovered that the majority of the them were the most civilized people you could ever meet. Ever since then, I have become very keen on overweight women and very thin women, small women and big women, young and old, and that class amongst them that wear glasses or who are crippled.

Right down to today, these women are by far my favourite type. And ever since then, when I spot a pretty-looking woman in the street, it comes to me that Sorley treated me very shoddily back then—how he left me clueless about the type of women I should have been going for from day one. In fact, I've found myself in a bit of a quandary ever since as regards women. How come I'm not always chasing the best-looking ones, the same as all the other men? And the answer is a simple one: I learned at quite a young age that every woman has her own beautiful and interesting attributes. This is a knowledge or an insight that the young men of today are not privy to anymore, given current attitudes and trends. Yet, despite this, the mores of this age in which we live dictate that it is young men who have to choose between the different types of women. Even the women themselves get very narky with you if they see that a man always goes for a certain type *per se*... But sure, what can you do!

Chapter 12

There was one night when, having circuited the hall, Sorley did not spot even one female face that wasn't bright and happy-looking! You would have thought that he'd be delighted with my efforts, wouldn't you? But no, not at all!

"Wouldn't it be at truly Christian act for someone to have a chat with that poor misfortunate sitting over there—look at her—mumbling away to herself. Isn't it really a horrible thing for a stranger to come into an Irish-language event only to be ignored like that? Not only is it unfriendly and downright rude but it's the opposite of everything Gaelic"

"Sorley, that's not a woman, that's a man!"

"What? What! A man? A woman? Sure, sex has nothing to do with it. All I can see is another lonely and troubled human soul. If someone would only have the chat with them?"

"You talk to them so Sorley!" I says.

Ara, I'm not used to just striking up a conversation with anyone at all—unless I've been introduced to someone beforehand! Sure, you're way more used to that sort of thing aren't you?"

I got up and walked over. Now, I don't know dear reader whether you've ever had this experience before. I don't know whether the same has happened to you as happened to me once—in the toilet of a very posh house belonging to some people I didn't know. Didn't I pull the bloody tap off the top of the sink by accident and next thing, the water was spraying out all over the place, and I couldn't jam it back into place again!

Well, this is exactly how I felt the first time I ever talked to the Foreign Professor. The chat just exploded out of him and sprayed all over the place like water from a burst mains. Everyone turned around suddenly and stared at me as much as to say that I'd just done something shameful or embarrassing! Straight away, I was angry with Sorley for sending me over to this fellow and I was angry with myself for not refusing Sam's request. Worse still, I was angry with this Professor fellow for the fact that I had to go and chat with him in the first place!

"Can you see the creature I mean? The fellow over there with the two eyes spinning in his head!" says Sorley.

And this was how I got to know the Foreign Professor the first day ever.

An oddball? He was as odd as the Grey Heron! As odd as the March Hare! And he was as lively as a windmill!

"It's nice," I says, trying to make conversation with him, "to look at the young people dancing, isn't it?"

"Maybe so," he says with a tormented look, "but have you ever seen the courtship dance of the woodcock? I prefer that to any human form of dancing?"

Already, people were sidling towards us trying to listen in on our conversation.

"The eldest chick in the sparrow-hawk's nest frequently devours the youngest fledgling. This happens while the mother-bird is too far away from the nest to intervene and it is usual for the sparrow hawk to hunt across quite a wide range of terrain. That said, it is a fact that the other species of birds don't receive as much care or training as do the fledglings of the birds of prey generally. The case of the sparrow-hawk aside, adult birds of prey are usually the most steadfast when it comes to looking after their chicks—the young eagles learning from

100

both their parents, flying and hunting alongside them for three months.—the young cock does his time alongside his mother helping her with hatching the eggs. It is true that in the case of the peregrine falcon, the father can't do very much for the fledglings if the mother dies; all of the chicks are in danger in dying from hunger in such circumstances.

Then, the eagle chicks spend a full three months learning everything alongside both their parent.

By now, a small crowd had gathered around us—whether to be friendly or not, I'm not entirely sure. But the Professor had moved on from birds to flowers and plants and was discussing the texture of cowslip juice with a sketch he drew with pen and paper. And the same then with the silverweed and the cuckooflower, even if I sensed that few of his listeners would've known the difference between an ox-eye daisy and a nettle.

But what was really bothering him the most was that he didn't have the correct Irish-language term for the *Viburnum rhytidophyllum*.

Next thing, some of the people at the céilí got mad with the Professor because he was spouting and blathering too much Irish. One man said and that it was not lucky to be too educated. Another said that too much knowledge sucks the physical energy out of people. There was talk of different people around the country who had lost their sanity because of too much education. One of the women was very critical of the Professor. A man who was always blathering on about the birds of the sky, how could you ever trust him?

I also realized then that he was one of those people whom Brendan O'Worried had warned me about—the crowd who'd travelled too far down the Irish language road.

Chapter 13

Shortly after I got to know the Foreign Professor we had an incident that was a bit of an embarrassing incident in relation to the band for the céilí. By then, we had a bad name amongst the city's musical fraternity, especially amongst the Irish music crowd. Back then. The Irish language crowd didn't pay a whole lot of attention (as many of the younger Irish language crowd do nowadays) to rock music, even if the same scene was beginning to grow and develop at the time. Rock was rarely was rarely mentioned in Irish-speaking circles other than to make little of it. But the rock afficionadoes existed and I was aware of them and so too did that group of their followers known as the "Hells Angels." I shouldn't have mentioned the rock music crowd to Sorley at all seeing as he was struggling to get musicians to try and keep the céilís going at the time.

"That's a really good idea!" he says.

"Aye," I says. But what about the Angels?"

"Who are they?"

I could tell that he'd never heard of the Angels before and that it wasn't worth the trouble trying to explaining them to him. So they went ahead and arranged a date for a gig with a certain rock group. I got an uneasy feeling up and down my spine when I first laid eyes on those musicians however. I don't remember whether there was much talk of punks at the time or of heavy metal either but the First Guitar in this group was dressed like a pirate while the second guitar was wearing a Nazi outfit. The Drummer had a right wild punk-look about him—he had the look of someone who'd slit your throat if you looked sideways at him! And they piled enough heavy metal on-stage around the Sound Man to start a small war!

The gig took place and it proved as disastrous an evening as ever seen in the history of the Gaelic League. I went across to the musicians at once stage:

"I think that there's been some sort of a misunderstanding," I says.

"A misunderstanding?"

"Yeah. A misunderstanding. You thought there was supposed to be a dance here tonight, didn't you, that you lads were lined up to play dance-music?

"Yeah. What do you mean? What are you saying anyway!"

There's no dance meant on here at all tonight, that's where the misunderstanding is. We have a University Professor lined up who's giving a lecture on the history of dance in ancient Ireland. The Nazi-looking Second Guitar Nancy threw his head back and burst out laughing at this. The drummer didn't see anything funny about it however.

"Were you crowd trying to make idiots of us?" he said menacingly.

"Where's this University Professor of yours then, anyway?" says the First Guitar.

I pushed the Foreign Professor forward:

"You're grand to give a lecture on dance this evening aren't you?" I says.

"Of course! Of course! I'll be speaking on the courtship dance of the woodcock"

The Second Guitar thought this was hilarious and roared with laugter again but the Sound Man didn't and pulled a knife on me instead, waving it in my face.

"You'll be hearing from us shortly again" the Drummer said threateningly as they packed up their stuff and left. On the way out the Banjo flung a chair at the window but missed. They were all threats as they left: "This isn't the end of this. We'll be back, guaranteed!"

Chapter 14

And sure enough, they sent a group of the Angels around come the next social organized in the hall. A bunch of lads, intent on wrecking the place. As the old proverb goes however: "The Devil looks after his own," and luckily for us the Angels turned up on the wrong night and to the wrong Grand Céilí—a dance that'd been organized by a group who had no connection with us. (I think that it was the Rowing Club's branch of the Railway Workers' Union that had organized the céilí that night.)

So, thankfully, we managed to emerge from that particular crisis unscathed.

The outcome of that incident was—what else?—that Sorley and the Baroness decided the Foreign Professor should give a public lecture. They wanted to see whether this proved more successful than some of the céilís they had organized. And, sure enough, the lecture went very well. On arriving at the hall that evening, I was worried about how it would go and next thing, I met two former novice nuns leaving the building just as I was going in.

"Am I late? Is the lecture over?"

"No! No! It has only just started. We didn't want to hear any more of it!"

"Why?"

"Sex! All he's going on about is sex! That lecturer! That fellow, he's been on about sex, since he was knee-high to a grasshopper!"

On hearing that word "sex" I burst through the main door into the hall with such speed that I hurt one person and broke two chairs into the bargain. As the whole world knows, sex was banned everywhere in Ireland during those years and it was the most difficult subject in life to get any accurate information about—whether in Irish or English. The younger crowd today should just be happy that they're here at all! If they knew just how clueless their parents on these issues, it's amazing that they came into the world at all! It is a bit of miracle really to tell you the truth! The way I saw it, it would be an awful pity to miss out on even one minute of a lecture on this subject, given that it was so rarely discussed and so I half-stumbled and half-staggered as I forced my way through the crowd up to a seat in the front row. Once everything had calmed down again, the Foreign Professor continued with his lecture:

"Prior to coupling, the seagulls bow to one another and make a noise that is very similar to a human laugh. The female opens her beak so that the male can give her some food but sometimes there isn't real food involved at all and it is a mock-ritual where he is feeding her and she is accepting his gift. A similar form of pretence goes on amongst terns with the cock flying on the wing pretending that he has a fish in his beak and the hen pursuing him to have some food. The terns also do a good deal of marching around as well as fluttering their wings and scratching the ground with their claws. As regards storm petrels, I'm not sure that there's a lot I can tell you about their activities and what they get up to when out of sight of the rest of us. It is in a hole in the ground that cock and hen do their coupling and courting, the details of which they keep to themselves and out of sight of others.

As for the godwits and curlews, the male flutters his wings while giving a high-pitched cry, a cry that's given solely on that occasion. I've often heard that unique cry of theirs: "I'll get you! I'll get you! I'll get you!"

That's what it sounds like. And it's what it means too! Having issued his cry, the cock chases the hen across the ground and when they tire of the chase, they play leap-frog with one another until it's time for sleep. As for the shags and the cormorants all they do is stretch their long necks a bit before they begin coupling. The lecture continued in this vein for ages until he had described every bird that has ever existed!

Chapter 15

From what I've recounted so far, you can see that there were many bright and learned people walking the Dublin streets at this juncture. If I come across to yourselves as being as bright as any of them—I won't refuse your assessment of me either! What is important is that you understand just how common unusual views and strange thoughts and philosophies were then amongst the residents of the capital.

The Gospels say that one should never call your brother a fool (even if he actually is one!) The way I see it—the day will come when the term "fool" won't be considered a term of disparagement at all,—and the people considered odd, or having strange views—or who are half-crazy itself—will be viewed in a much different light. When that day comes, it will be recognized everywhere that to be deemed a "fool" is not a criticism at all but rather the exact opposite—i.e. a form of praise. Because the day will come when the entire world will be subject to the same standardized, generalized form of thinking and philosophy as imposed on everyone, everywhere, in a way that is both compulsory and incomprehensible at the same time. This sameness or homogenous view of the world will drown us all like the enormous tides that invade our coastlines each day, filling every cove and bay. This is the time when those brave souls who didn't agree or assent to all the attitudes and views that were current and fashionable in their day will be sought out—those unique individuals that ploughed their own furrow—in their own rough or eccentric way, the people who tried to escape the stifling tidal wave of crazy conformity, sameness, and group-think that overwhelmed the world—just as Noah and his Ark rode out the Flood and emerged safely on the other side. Mark my words! Every race and people will be crying out for such people when that day comes around!

Nowadays, the man who tells us he knows exactly what's going on is really saying just how completely lost he is in reality! The pigeons that eat the grains of bread off the paths and streets see no shame in their ignorance regarding the workings of the flourmill. It isn't in our gift either to comprehend this world in all its fullness—no more than the pigeons can.

I described earlier how things were from an educational point of view in the old school (not that I'm trying to make little of the school or undermine it as occurred when I was running the school—but anyway...)

The truth is that in those days the curriculum wasn't much to write home about in Irish schools—whatever it was like in other countries. The more I got to know my peers from other parts of Ireland, including youngsters from Dublin, the more I realised that we were all in the same boat back then when it came to schooling. Education at the time was based on the idea that the schools existed to revive theories and ideas that were old-hat, worn-out or dead, and re-orient these failed approaches in line with modern Irish society. Inspired by this concept of education, people could've been forgiven for thinking that a child's mind was like a dustbin into which you forced a huge variety of thoughts and subjects. What the teaching fraternity were most concerned with then was just offloading these latest products of the educational system—products that were no longer required—either within their own country or through their emigration abroad—as quickly as possible. To what extent each child understood the hotchpotch of ideas and theories they learned was entirely up to themselves. And this is what left the Irish people blind and ignorant of what was happening to them—the same as cows in the lorry making for the abattoir.

One aspect of life in those days that no one would believe you about—if you described it to them nowadays—was the following:

Handing a one-pound note to the barman and asking him for a pint—and him waiting for the second pound note from you before he put his hand on the tap at all. I'm not going to say that we didn't have economic problems back then because we did. I'm not going to say either that the ruling class wasn't as keen as ever to focus the public's attention on the political stage while ignoring other issues—because they were! But they weren't as successful with that strategy back then as they are today. The economy? The attitude that most people had back then was this: what you didn't know or understand, you were better off not bothering about. Just because the devil was asking for you didn't mean you had to go looking for him. How well myself and Sorley ran into each other when we did, you might say! It was Sorley who explained the economic system to me—and I am grateful to him a thousand times over for this too. I can never thank him enough either for the way that he explained class warfare to me. It was after I'd heard the full story about the oppression and injustice being perpetrated on the working class from him that I decided to side with capitalism. These days, they refer to every dispute and disagreement between people as a misunderstanding but there's been many a fine agreement between people over the years that was based on nothing more than a misunderstanding. Everyone taking their own meaning from the agreement so to speak!

Such was the arrangement that I preferred to have with Sorley—and provided we never actually assigned terms to our agreement, everything went grand. But then, don't they say that the seed of every great dispute lies in the moment when people understand one another fully and clearly? If it wasn't for Sorley, I'd never have thought of having an office of my own in Dublin. Not that he recommended this idea in the first place. Forking out rent for an office and making out that I was a businessman was something that Socialist Sorley would never have been able to get his head around. Indeed, if I'd been asked the question myself the day I decided to have an office of my own and enter the world of trade and commerce—I'd have been confused myself as to what a businessman actually did. I'd have been left standing there like a right idiot.

I wanted an office of my own with a desk and a chair and my name inscribed on some kind of plaque on the door outside. Inside on the desk I'd have an in-tray with "In" marked on it and an out-tray with "Out" marked on it. The way I saw it—I had as much right to this under the Irish Constitution as any clerk or desk official anywhere in the city of Dublin.

If it is generally acknowledged that bureaucracy is a Socialist disease so what's the harm in me admitting that I'd been struck down with it the same as small children get sick with the measles or with are the mumps? The bureaucracy disease isn't the sort of thing that makes someone take to their bed but rather their chair instead. It's not that you're forced to lie down with the illness but rather to sit down with it. Or maybe the bug I got was the normal hankering for an office that is common to many people these days. A characteristic of mine was always to ignore the guidance of my elders completely, or to seek out their advice either—or even to make my own of their words of wisdom. If only someone had been there to educate me on Sigmund Freud… to explain the meaning of psychology in the same way that Sorley had educated me about Marx and socialism…

Chapter 16

I got my own office anyway. It might have been small but at least it was in the centre of the city and within an ass' roar of the General Post Office. Even if it was situated high on the ninth floor just beneath the roof of the building. And even if it was bare and very basic, the rent on it was only 12 shillings a week and sixpence a week. I got a timber board and some paint and after much thought and effort, I came up with the following sign and personal testament for display- "CONSOLIDATED GAELIC HOLDINGS LIMITED.

AGENT: Harrigan Hassle (9th Floor)

Once I'd picked a spot and secured the sign to the front entrance of the building down below, I went back upstairs to my nest on the 9th floor to check it out. I'm not sure whether I need to explain this to yourselves—the young people of today—but there is always a positive hidden in every negative or misfortune, even if it isn't clear to us initially.

On the surface of it, having an office on the ninth floor of a building without an elevator might have appeared a major negative. It was only the rare customer that would have had it in them to attack the nine floors of that stairs to do business with me there but, on the other hand, it was only the rare debt collector who'd undertake the same climb either—and only if they had someone on their list of debtors.

My new post high up near the roof was a lonely-enough station seeing as mine was the only office on that floor. The office might have been small and cramped but at least I'd the benefit of knowing that no one would bother making the trek up past the 8th floor unless they'd important or essential business with me. (On realizing this, I went back downstairs as far as the 7th floor where I attached a simple electrical device or buzzer to warn me as soon as anyone made for the top floor.)

Anyway, a full three weeks went by before another human being called to the office seeking my services—albeit that the owner of the building visited me once. The latter had to sit down on my chair for twenty minutes to catch his breath, then explained in an irritated tone that it wasn't worth his while climbing so many steps of stairs to collect his miserable, little, 12/6 a week from me! He told me that I'd have to arrange to pay the rent on an annual basis with another tenant on one of the floors below—that they could take the money from me and then pass it onto him. I agreed that such an arrangement would be easier for both of us and he left the office again with a half satisfied snort.

A week went by and then another, and I began to get used to the idea that the Irish public couldn't have cared less whether "CONSOLIDATED GAELIC HOLDINGS" existed or not.

Chapter 17

In my little cell of an office, I had a habit of sitting on the desk, my feet perched on the chair from where I'd look out across the roofs of the capital towards the statue of Horatio Nelson.

I didn't know then, of course, that Nelson wouldn't be stood on his plinth there for too many more years. If I'd known that at the time, it might've proved a great consolation to me, but anyway...). At that juncture in time, I was slightly jealous and in awe of the man to tell you the truth. A man who'd been dead for 150 years and people were still happy to pay 10 pence and climb hundreds of steps up a stone stairs just to get a close look at his image. And the same people wouldn't do business with me and I was still alive and kicking! My only flaw being that I was on the 9th floor!

I was sitting at my desk one day reflecting on this injustice when the buzzer sounded, indicating that some creature— whether human or supernatural—had passed up beyond the 8th floor. I hopped off the desk, sat into my chair, and began scribbling fiercely—"DEAR SIR, DEAR SIR, "DEAR BLOODY SIR." A moment later and I heard a light knock on the door.

"Come in! Come in!" I says, appearing very officious. "Come in and sit down!"

A big, rough-looking lump of a man with pointy ears came in; sporting a fine well-cut suit; he had the look of a farmer on a rare visit to the city. He stepped through the door slowly and carefully, his eyes looking me up and down; half-smiling, he scanned the small office, then took a seat and smiled benevolently across the desk at me.

"Maybe I can do something for you?" I says.

"I don't think so. I'm looking for some information" he says.

"Information. What sort of information would that be?"

"I'd like to ask you a few questions."

"For some strange reason, a shiver of anxiety ran up my spine from somewhere down in the seat of my pants."

"I see that you're "CONSOLIDATED" he says... how does that feel... to be "CONSOLIDATED," I mean?"

To be "CONSOLIDATED" is just like anything else. Someone who's consolidated feels exactly the same as they felt before they reached this status or station. In the same way as an upper class gentleman has the same physical feelings as the man who has little or no status worth talking about.

"I see," he says, as much as to say that this half-baked, ridiculous explanation of mine was sufficient for him.

"And you're "LIMITED" also, aren't you?"

"Aren't we all limited in some way or another? Is there any man, woman or child in this world who isn't limited in some way?"

"But you're not a limited company yourself, that's the point isn't it?" he says, raising his voice slightly. "And what about your HOLDINGS? Where are they?"

I glanced at my desk and my chairs and then over at the picture of the girl on the calendar that I'd received free from a local car dealer.

"There are "HOLDINGS"... and then there are "HOLDINGS" I says, becoming annoyed.

"Excuse me, my friend, but have you come here just to mock me? What business do you have with me here or who do you work for?" I says. He gave me a serious look then handed me

115

a card across the desk on which the following words were printed:

"The Fraud Squad, Dublin Castle."

"What are you accusing me of exactly? Okay, I'll tell you. I thought of calling my failed attempts at reviving our country's economy 'CONSOLIDATED GAELIC HOLDINGS'. Can someone not refer to themselves as an 'AGENT' without breaking some law or other?"

"Who are you working for as an agent? Which international company sent you to Dublin on their behalf? he asked. "You shouldn't claim to be a limited company when you're not registered as a limited company and the same goes for 'CONSOLIDATED'. If you claim to have 'HOLDINGS', there's a good chance you'll be asked to prove this through showing invoices to this effect.

"Am I even allowed to say that I'm 'GAELIC' itself?" I asked.

"I don't care about you being 'Gaelic'," he says, "because I've nothing to do with the political squad. Our department has no interest whatsoever in politics.

"That said, I find it odd that a businessman would attract attention to himself by using a words like Gaelic. Unless you're in the IRA, are you? It's not the business of our department anyway, one way or the other," he says, rising from his seat to leave.

"God Almighty!" I says. "You're not going to charge me with something, are you? Or what's the story?"

"No. But, we will be keeping an eye on how you get on in the long term" he concluded. And off he went.

I thought things over for a few minutes, then went and got a brush and paint, and began working on the ground-floor sign outside, where I painted over the words "CONSOLIDATED GAELIC HOLDINGS LIMITED", wiping them from the face of the world. I left the word "GAELIC" there until the very end and then daubed over it with black paint. All that was left on the sign then was HARRIGAN HASSLE AGENT (9th Floor).

How many people before me had this same word GAELIC caused such great heartbreak for?

Chapter 18

They say that the world is changing but people are always changing too and often in a way other than how they might wish to. Take Socialist Sorley, for example. His explanation of all the injustices the workers were suffering—this was what prompted me to take an office for myself in Dublin city centre in the first place. From that point on, I sought to be associated with the commercial and capitalist class, rather than those who were suffering or oppressed. I was grateful to Sorley for explaining economics to me so that I was amongst the small number of people back then who understood that such a thing as an economy actually existed.

As for Whiny Maolchú, it wasn't economics as we understand it that he went on about mostly.

"The thing that's wrong with the Irish Language Movement is…" he'd say over and over again. He'd say the same thing every day of the year. He'd say it twenty times a week and more… And I had reason to be grateful that he couldn't visit me as often as he'd have liked as the building was locked every Bank Holiday and Sunday. So Whiny called into me every Monday, Tuesday and Wednesday. He called on Thursdays because that was when he received a few shillings from the employment exchange in Denmark Street. Money that the government deemed worth giving him on the one condition—that he took no hand or part in the economic or industrial expan-

118

sion of the country. To give Whiny his due he was quite happy to obey these conditions and for as long as I had any dealings with him, he never took anything stronger than a pint of Guinness. He never bothered me on a Friday or a Saturday either because he spent both those days down in the bookies.

Not that he was that fond of bookies or anything. In fact, he considered them all rogues and gangsters, Enemies of the People, the ruination of the Nation! What brought him to the betting office was that he actually had a scheme laid out, a massive scam that, if successful, would have put all the bookies in the Poorhouse forever—(something that they richly-deserved!). I have to admit that I took no part in this scheme of his, even if to give him his due, he invited me to get in on it—on the "ground floor"—as he put it. I told him that he was the heart and soul of generosity—but seeing as he himself had come up with the scheme and had put so much time and effort into it— it'd have been right blackguardry on my part to slip in the back door on it and take the bit from his mouth at the last minute. He himself should have all the profit from it, I told him. Of course, it's understood that when it comes to commercial matters, there is always a degree of bluster and con-artistry going on. So that it is not always clear who's trying to fool who in the end!

Whatever free time Whiny had left over—after his researches on greyhound racing and the horses were done—he was happy to sacrifice it by proclaiming the weaknesses and shortcomings of the Irish Language Movement to the rest of the world.

Whoever told you that Whiny Maolchú was a first-class pain in the arse wasn't far wrong, I can assure you! How I put up with him and his oddities for as long as I did, I'll never know! What got into me to let him into my office the first day ever— only God knows. If I wanted to get ahead in life as a big-city businessman, I didn't have time to waste on a ne'er-do-well the likes of Whiny in fairness, now did I?

The explanation for this lies in the strange circumstances I found myself in at the time. I was beginning to think that I would never have any customers at all—not unless you include people who were seeking immediate payment for products that they'd delivered years ago.

At the top of the list was the rent-man who never saw the colour of my money from the day that I first paid the deposit and rented the office. Other big customers of mine—in that sense of the word—were Dublin Corporation who wanted to raise some question about rates with me—also, the Water Board, the Gas Board and the Energy Supply Board. In fact, I was worn-out and sick to death of the uniformity of attitudes they all showed me. From the way they went on, you'd have thought that there was nothing more important in this world.

This was why I welcomed Whiny Maolchú the first time he called in. Not only did he speak Irish but he was very worried about the Irish Language Movement, the same issue that frequently dominated my own thoughts. "The thing that's wrong with the Irish Language Movement is…"

There were occasions after this when I enjoyed his company needless to say. Part of the problem was that the buzzer no longer went off and warned me that someone had reached the steps of the eighth floor. Whiny had such long legs that he could climb the stairs very quickly, three steps at a time. As a result, he'd arrive in the office door when I wasn't expecting him at all and sometimes he didn't even wish me the time of day, he was in such a mad rush to promulgate his theories and propaganda.

"The thing that's wrong with the Irish Language Movement is…" he'd say, blurting out whatever speech he'd thought up on the way over there—or in bed before getting up for the day—"The thing that's wrong…"

Sometimes, he'd focus his ire on me like a rebel soldier taking someone out in a burst of gunfire. "The thing that's wrong…"

Other times, he appeared again like an expert sharpshooter sniping the target and promptly disappearing from sight again. Other times again, he'd be deep in thought and there wasn't a word out of him as he quietly prepared his next bout of speechifying. On these latter occasions, he'd always plonk his disagreeable lump of a self between me and whatever light streamed in from the skylight above—a fact which made me realize that maybe they weren't the worst really—the electricity people: even if wouldn't supply me with any light until I agreed to pay the bill.

Now, I had nothing against the Electricity Supply Board at all and let no one say that I did. I never considered the price of electricity too high or anything like that either. I've always considered all of the electricity suppliers a reasonable and humane crowd and their rates as very reasonable—and that's the end of it.

Chapter 19

Back then, the sole bone of contention between me and the electricity suppliers was that I had no intention of paying their bills. Anyway, even in the month of January, some light always came in through the window between half-10 in the morning and 4 o'clock in the afternoon; and if I was really hard-pressed, I could shift all of my office-work over to the public library or the National Gallery or to a park bench or Saint Dominic's Church.

Having studied the question carefully, it became clear to me that there was no point paying any electricity bills—not until I was out of the financial doldrums and solvent anyway. I'd have time enough to be thinking of paying electricity bills once I'd come through the economic downturn. This is not to say that I was happy with Whiny Maolchú drinking my tea and stealing my daylight and deafening me with his lectures about the Irish Language Movement. One day as he raised his arm to drain the last few drops of tea from the pot, I gruffly asked him: "So, what's wrong with the Irish Language Movement anyway?" and this stopped him in his tracks. After a moment's hesitation, he said in a faltering voice that was unusual for him—that many of the language crowd did not get on with another. "That's not a bad answer," I said to myself. Because—even if he was an Irish-language enthusiast, as I was—as we both were—I still couldn't stand him at times.

I hated the way he always appeared just as I'd the tea made, and proceeded to drink the whole pot on me, cup after cup. And I hated the way he settled his tall frame between me and the weak light that tried to make its way through the skylight to illuminate my dreary little office on cold winter mornings. It is true that for a while I suspected some of the Irish language crowd had done something on him that turned him against them. But this wasn't it, as it turns out.

Those words of his that he always repeated were just his badge of identity, similar to the sound that a bird or an animal makes—as if to indicate its presence. "The thing that's wrong with the Irish Language Movement is that…" as Whiny Maolchú used to say. It was his salutation, his signature tune. To be fair to him, Whiny had had positive views of his own about the language situation at one time. God knows, he had listened to many long hours of debate and discussion on the problems of the Irish Language Movement in his time. And it was after a good deal of deep reflection on the issue that his views on the shortcomings of the Irish Language Movement had formed earlier. But the complexity of the arguments and his love of porter and his general exhaustion with the whole thing, his insights had dulled over time.

It occurred to me just then that the entire Irish public, myself included, were beholden to this individual who gone out of his way to make sure we were all aware of the issue that obsessed him and tormented him in equal measure. He had made the language question centre-stage and placed it right before her eyes so that no one could ignore it anymore. He ensured that the language question was dissipated everywhere into the atmosphere—much the same as the dandelion scatters its seeds everywhere on the summer air. He'd done a great service by posing the question that every Gaeilgeoir in the country had to make sense of in their own way at some point in their lives… The thing that's wrong with the Irish Language Movement is:

123

There was one morning however when I was ready for him. I had a big, bulky German-made tape recorder under the desk (The Japanese model didn't become popular until a few years later.) I thought to myself that I'd save a sample of some of Whiny Maolchú's mad pronouncements for future generations so that they'd know what type of people were around in 1957. Anyway, to make a long story short, Whiny arrived in and he was in fine fettle and spouting off and lecturing and whining about this that and the other. And I got the whole lot down on tape.

Once he was gone, I rewound the tape and listened back carefully to what he'd said. I had a pen and paper at the ready to make notes. The whole thing turned out to be a major disappointment however and I wasn't long realizing that the whole thing from beginning to end was nothing but a load of rubbish—the biggest pile of empty talk and waffle—and not as much as one positive hope or sentiment expressed by him from beginning to end.

There was any amount of "On the other hand" and "If you look at the question the issue this way…" and "having examined the issue carefully…" Another phrase he used regularly was "in the heel of the hunt…" He said the latter 11 times during the course of his speech. I wouldn't have minded but at no stage—not even once—did he come anywhere within an ass's roar of "at the end of the day."

No doubt about it but Whiny Maolchú was a real one-tune piper. "The thing that's wrong with the Irish Language Movement…" were the first words from his mouth every time he sat his backside down in my office high above the roofs of Dublin city. "The thing that's wrong with the Irish Language Movement…"

So that in the end I decided that he himself, this man who made his way through the streets of Dublin each day—was the living embodiment of what he meant by that endless refrain of

124

his—as spouted day and night from one end of the year the other. I wrote down a list of his qualifications for this role—as if to commemorate his legacy even while he was still alive—his was the enumeration of the *Seven Illusions* that were the ruination of the Irish Language Brigade of our time:

Letting down Friends
Narrowness of vision
A Fondness for Boring Issues
An Expectation of Failure
Being a Complete Lazy-Arse
The Avoidance of Reality
The Provision of False Information

Part 3

Chapter 1

It is with great difficulty that I begin this part of my story. As I'm afraid that no one will believe me. Because the events I outline here are so unusual and bizarre that I'm often tempted to erase them from my memory. That said, it would be a major loss to the Gaelic community if the full story wasn't recorded for posterity. Time is passing very quickly and none of us are getting any younger; instead, we are aging day by day. From when I first got to know Whiny Maolchú, I never once saw him hesitate in his sermonizing relating to the Irish language. Not until this one incredible day that I'm about to tell you about. This was the first miracle in a day that was full of miracles.

Whiny had his back to the window as usual that day and his face to the door that was wide-open—as the weather was very close. One minute, he was spouting away to his heart's content about the Irish language,—while I focussed on my work and tried to block out his ramblings—the next he fell deathly silent, his mouth agape at something in the passageway outside—I looked up from my work in amazement at the sudden cessation in his stream of waffle. I'd always assumed that nothing could ever stop Whiny Maolchú suddenly in his tracks when he was on a roll about Irish.

A burly low-sized block of a woman rushed into the room her skin the colour of burnished oak, her hair dark-black and frizzy. She was dressed in military uniform and looked right through Whiny as much as to say—"Will you ever get out of my way?" She grabbed Whiny by the scruff of the neck and flung him across the room with a flick of her powerful wrist—as if he wasn't even there. Bursting in on her heels came another woman from the same race who proceeded to open a small handbag and assemble a rifle of the most modern type with swiftly and with great expertise. She hopped onto my desk, clambered up through the skylight as nimble as a cat and was out on the roof. Whatever she was looking for out there must have been to her satisfaction because she climbed back into the room again a few seconds later where two other women from the same group had appeared, one of whom took a handgun from her rucksack and examined it carefully. The other much taller woman had no gun, I think, but she suddenly she pulled out a long and vicious-looking knife out—it must have been at least 10 inches long—and turned to me at the desk where I was still in a daze. She went on her hunkers and placed her two elbows on the desk, then pointed the blade in my face a half-inch from my moustache. Moving the blade slowly from side to side: left, right, left, right, she stared into my eyes and said slowly and deliberately in a strange dialect that I'd never heard before in my life:

"Am… friotal… du… galen?"[2]

Anyone who doesn't believe that they have a guardian angel doesn't deserve to have one… And I'm not sure where my response came from but it did…

"Ya! Ya! Friotal mi Galen, I sure do!"

The rebel got to her feet and pulled the knife back from my face, even if my eyes remained fixed on its flashing blade. Her blade whirled before me as if slicing the air into slivers, its fierce dagger whirling and twirling as if dancing with joy.

---

2   'Um… expression… *thou*… Galish?'

These mysterious and wonderful women let a series of loud whoops and roars of exultation out of them, as if proclaiming their joy to whoever else was still outside in the stairwell:

"Friotal Gaelainne aquí!"[3]

and

"Hablan Gaeilge,a mháithair!"[4]

and

"Párlaítear Tengluan/Tlenguan irin indemne!"[5]

Next, a fourth woman arrived in, a large woman with a proud, noble bearing, a stately-looking woman, a woman in every sense of the word. The woman with the blade suddenly grabbed me in a bear-hug (she nearly broke my back... but anyway!) then pointed the blade at Whiny Maolchú, to where he was still lying half-crumpled against the wall.

"Galen friotal é chomh maith?"[6]

Sorley seemed to have been hurt badly after being smashed against the wall—his mouth was open-wide, his eyes staring blankly ahead—you'd have thought he was half-dead!

I says: "For absolutely certain, he speaks excellent Gaeilge Galeneach Gaelainneach Gaeltheangach Éireannachúil!"[7] I was put to the pin of my collar but did my best to provide the rebels with a clear and intelligible response, focusing in particular on the female warrior with the long knife. Whether rightly or wrongly they accepted my word at face value even if I admit that I was angry and very jealous on seeing all the petting and mollycoddling of Whiny Maolchú they got up to afterwards.

---

3   'Expression of Gaeling *aquí*.'

4   '*Hablan* Irish, O mother!'

5   'One parleys Tengluan/Tlenguan something something!'

6   'Does he expression Galish as well?'

7   'For absolutely certain, he speaks excellent Irish Galish Gaelingish Gael-lingual Irelandishic!'

Chapter 2

They were rough enough with him in the beginning…
prodding and shaking him…then shoving him around the
room from one woman to the next. They were like girls playing
with a football or a cat playing with a mouse. In the meantime,
a little smirk appeared on his face—(the shameless devil!)

There is a therapeutic or healing power in the tips of a
woman's fingers—not only that, but the gift of prophecy or
foresight comes naturally to them. Attempts are made to stifle
these abilities in the women of Ireland through over-education
however. Yet, these unique abilities and traits live on in our
womenfolk all the same. So that it didn't take too long for these
miraculous women, wherever they were from originally—to
identify where Whiny Maolchú was hurt and to provide the
patient with appropriate and intense healing. They now put all
their energies into tending to him, one woman after another,
each of them in their turn. Whiny was their experiment, as
they worked their therapy on him—it was nearly as if they were
performing some type of ritual or exorcism on him and there
was no letting them him go until they'd done everything they
could to heal him.

And I could see that he was really enjoying this *regimen*
despite himself, his face creased up in a great wrinkled smile.
For a while, it looked as if he mightn't come through the ther-

apy safely at all but he eventually came to himself and recovered.

The Eskimos, the nation that make their home in the region of eternal snow, they have understood since ancient times that there's nothing better in the world to revive the body heat in someone who's suffered hypothermia than plenty of female company and a few days of female touch.

They managed to revive Whiny anyway and even I'm not qualified enough to say that this operation proved a complete success, there's no doubt about it but that there was marked improvement in their patient. He was the old Whiny Maolchú no longer. He'd always been a bit odd but now he was strange in a completely different way. The issues that used to bother him prior to this were now a great source of humour to him instead. Where once, the Irish-language crowd had tried to avoid him completely given his ever-bleak prognosis regarding the language—now they continued to avoid him because of his bizarre, new habit of exploding with laughter right in the middle of a meeting.

The therapy these women applied to him is one—not all of the experts agreed as to when it was first practiced by human beings. And I don't know either who was the first nurse to practice it on someone or who their first patient was either. But as far back as it's possible to go in the history of humanity, it seems that women have been applying this therapy to men and men have been benefiting from it.

These Bronze-skinned angels who'd appeared up there to us as if from another world had found a poor Gaeilgeoir who'd travelled too far along the road of theory and over-analysis without anyone to tell him that it was a road without a destination. This was a road laid down for us by those who seek too beguile us and lead us astray, a road that doesn't lead anywhere at all. But there is some impulsive and restless spirit in the Irish language crowd whereby their own self-destruction is the always the outcome. And it would have taken more than a short and simple exorcism to extricate Maolchú from this particular problem. You needed more than a couple of women for this job—it needed a whole group working together.

The women stayed the night there along with Whiny and myself. Aye! In that miserable little office of mine! Between the office and tiny passageway outside, I don't know how we managed to find space enough for six people. The women had brought their own food with them, food that you only rarely saw anything similar to it on our side of the world back then. They had their own ways of preparing the food and their own cooking utensils that they'd brought with them also.

I was trying my best to understand the language they were speaking. It was a type of Irish without a doubt but it was the strangest Irish you could ever imagine. Given its non-European flavour and the fact that they had so many loan words from other languages in this Irish of theirs—I was mad keen to pick up some of it; and I couldn't wait to ask these women some questions. Where were they from? What had brought them to Ireland or what was their business here? How long would they be staying for? How had they travelled here?

Chapter 3

They stayed there for another twenty-four hours. They were very easy-going. It was clear that they were from a part of the world where it was no big deal what kind of a building you found yourself in, whether grand of small. Using a cramped little office on the ninth floor like mine—as your lodgings, sleeping quarters and military outpost all-in-one. As for the Knife Woman—she got a great kick out of letting things fall over the railings of the eighth floor and watching them tumble to the ground.

On the morning of the third day, the landlord of the building called around. "Someone's complained to me," he says, when I ran down to the sixth floor to meet him. I prayed that he wouldn't spot any of the women sitting on the stairs above eating a red mushy food of some description with their fingers out of clay bowls. He wasn't long noticing them however.

"Where are these people from?" he says.

"From Palumo," I says.

"From Palumbria. It's the name of a country—or a region of a country. Polombriano. It's situated between the Narrow Plain and the Dead Sea."

"And what are they doing over here?"

"They're a *trade delegation!*

"Hmm! And what will the neighbours here say about them, I wonder?"

THE MIGHTY WOMAN'S ADVENTURES ABROAD

"These people are new to the traditions and customs of this country. It's their first time in Ireland and their visit here is a great opportunity for us! It'll open up a whole host of new and wonderful possibilities. And they've a great demand for Irish-made products. There'll be big profits out of it!"

"Oh! You'll be able to pay the rent so!" he says, his eyes lighting up in anticipation.

"But, this is no time to be extravagant!" I says.

"There's a big need for credit right now" I says, rubbing the palms of my hands together in delight. "All in good time!" "A windy day is not a good day for thatching."

Whatever day it was anyway—it was the day that the women gathered their stuff together and said their goodbyes.

They all kissed Whiny and me before leaving, then kissed me again and then Whiny again. They even shed a few tears. And they spoke a great deal also. If only I'd been able to understand what it was they were saying! Whatever it was, I'm certain that they were repeating their message over and over again. We couldn't understand them however.

And that was it…

They were gone again and it was as if they'd never been there at all; and we knew so little about them. Other than that, the Blade Woman had left her mark behind. Just one word carved neatly into the timber floorboards!

(I had to buy a carpet mat to cover it so that the landlord didn't see it!) The word "Latachúnga" and the letters D.K.S.O.G. inscribed above it in capitals.

"What does 'Latachúnga' mean?" I said to Whiny Maolchú afterwards.

"I'm not sure, but they're the letters they kept repeating just before they left. Would it be the name of a place maybe? And what does D.K.S.O.G. mean also?

Chapter 4

I'm sitting at my desk one afternoon staring out in the direction of Horatio Nelson as usual when the buzzer goes off and I know that someone's on their way up. I quickly adopt a busy air about me and wait for the knock on the door. Who comes in's in but a big sturdy-looking lump of a man in a suit—a buck with the look of a country man on his first visit to the big city—it's Detective-Sergeant MacContrary.

I give him a great welcome. I'm all over him straight away, worshipping him and all the rest of it—then cut to the chase: "So, Inspector-General, your Worship, what can I do for you this time?"

He raised his hands to his face in false modesty. "I'm just a Detective-Sergeant. Don't give me a status that they haven't given me the high salary for!"

"But you might have that status and pay one of the day's yet? No one knows what lies around the corner. I heard about a man who was a limited company one day and the next, he had that status swiped from him!"

"That's a good one!" he says, with a short laugh.

"It's always good when the Garda Síochána have a sense of humour."

"That's what keeps them going," he says.

"That and the snake-milk they're always drinking!" I says, except that I didn't say that bit out loud! If we were to reveal our private thoughts in the presence of government officials, would freedom be on the march in so many parts of the world today? Maybe so. It probably wouldn't matter anyway in the case of the Guards because the police can read your mind anyway! In the case of the more astute policemen, they say that they can read your thoughts before you've even thought them yourself! The training that the police receive means that their entire focus on secrecy. Consequently, when you speak to the police, they're on a different wavelength to you really. One where the policemen can listen in on everything that's being said.

A hurt look clouded the man's face however.

"I only came down here to have a bit of crack with you."

"You thought I might be a bit lonely, is it?" I says.

"Exactly" he says. "I guessed there that there probably wouldn't be hordes of people climbing up those endless for the chat with you!"

My attitude softened towards him—even if no-one belonging to me—as far back through the generations as you can go—would've offered so much as a cup of water to any man who working for the government. The day eventually comes around when the most deep-set of traditions are broken and the most long established of attitudes no longer apply.

"You'll have a drink, will you?" I says.

He refused but it was obvious that his heart wasn't in it.

"Wait and I'll get us two glasses."

Once we were sitting comfortably with a drop of the hard stuff in our hands, he says:

"Isn't the Irish language the finest thing in the world? I think that there's probably nothing more beautiful in the world than to hear a man speaking his own language in all its melodic fluency?" he says.

"I thought you were always suspicious of the Irish language crowd!"

"Suspicious? Of Gaeilgeoirí is it? How do you mean?" he says, with a look of confusion.

"Sure, doesn't the President of Ireland always have Irish? Don't the clergy, the bishops, the government ministers, and the members of the Senate all have Irish?

The most devout and the cleverest and the brightest people in the country? How could the police possibly be suspicious of the Irish language brigade?"

He was taken aback by my claim.

"Well…" I says. "Hearing what you've just said has come as a big relief to me and I'll promise to spread the word amongst the Irish language community in Ireland and abroad. In all the places of sanctuary they frequent, they'll be only delighted to hear that they are no longer perceived as outlaws of the glens that have to remain out of sight from now on. You have no idea how much encouragement and hope your words will give to those people who always felt they had to hide themselves away in their underground hideouts and caves forever. Fearful of the experts who felt that they'd likely grow tall ears and develop eyes on the sides of their heads, the same as the hare— they were so used to fleeing the forces of law and government."

"On the other hand," says Detective-Sergeant MacContrary. You have to admit that the Irish Language Movement does attract some strange people to its ranks. People whom it is difficult to disregard!"

"So, what you're saying Sergeant is that—the Guards have to keep an eye on the Irish Language Movement all time, is it?"

"Look! It's like this," he says. "At the Apple Festival and any of the events you've held recently the Minister of State gave a speech and said that the Irish language is the most precious jewel the nation's possesses…"

"And there's nothing more important in the eyes of the police than keeping a close watch over our most valuable national jewel!" I says.

"Yes. There you have it. Spot-on," says the Sergeant. And we had a nice few drinks on that.

Chapter 5

Reflecting on the issue, the following thought struck me a short while later:

"It's all well and good you saying that the language is a priceless jewel of ours and this is why the police keep a close eye on her but it's not a precious gem—in the sense that a robber might steal it from a jewellers—or thieves from a bank—is it? It isn't a gem that hold-up men or burglars might steal through the use of violence or armed robbery is it? Consequently, how can our ancient language be such a source of concern and something that has to be carefully protected by yourselves in the police?"

"That's easy to explain," says Detective-Sergeant MacContrary. "Robbery, whether major or minor, or whether violent or no, has never been a subject of investigation for me as a policeman. In fact, I work for the Fraud Squad and the only crimes we're concerned with always have some element of fraud or deception in them."

I thought about this for a moment then suddenly I jumped up from my chair in anger.

"What are you saying here exactly? That this is subject to charge! You're ascribing fraud and deception to the Irish language enthusiasts, is it! The class of people who're the most innocent and saintly and the least materialistic people in the entire country! You'll be hearing from the Executive Committee about this Sergeant, I can guarantee you!"

This didn't knock a stir out of him however.

"Come on Hassle, you're not as innocent as you're letting on! Tell the truth now. Would *you* buy a used car from another Gaeilgeoir, would you?"

"That's nothing to do with it!" I says.

"All I'm mean is," he says slowly, "that people drift in and out of your language movement and their words and verbs prove Irregular in the Present Tense. Way too much in the way of howling and exclamation marks out of them!

In any country except Ireland, they'd be able to link their Declensions with the Copula properly. Some of them are far too given to the use of the Autonomous Verb in Indirect Speech!" I became more annoyed with him now. The veiled threat that lay behind his words! I didn't like it one bit and I whacked the table with my hand.

"Name them! Name them so!"

He shifted his glass to one side.

"Do you know Erfurt von Volcaniceruption?"

"God between us and all harm!"

I sat down.

"You obviously know who he is so?"

"I don't know him at all. I was only saying a prayer. Erfurt what? Anyone with a baptismal name like that deserves a few prayers!"

"Spell it, will you?"

"I can't. It's not Irish."

"You're telling me! It's as un-Gaelic as Queen Victoria's knickers—herself, whose statue was out in the park there before it was blown to bits."

"Don't mind the Queen's knickers, would you? That's not relevant."

And I sensed that he was getting a bit irked himself at the way this conversation was turning.

"Who'd have thought it?" I says, trying to get him onside a bit again, "that there could be anything untoward or odd relating to the Irish language."

"Well—it does relate to the Irish language in this case," says the Detective-Sergeant.

"Erfurt who?"

"Von Volcaniceruption!"

"What does he look like—in case I spot him at any stage?"

"He's one of the biggest men you've ever seen in your life!"

"You're fairly tall yourself Sergeant."

"This man is enormous. Seven feet tall at least. And huge wide shoulders on him. Do you have German?"

"Not much."

"Huh! Have you enough to make sense of this?"

He took a piece of paper from the desk and wrote something on it. It read:

"Deutsch-Keltische-Stiller-Ozean-Genossen.

It doesn't mean anything to me."

"Huh!" he says staring at me, unsure as to whether to believe me or not.

I was tempted to fling the piece of paper into the bin. Mac-Contrary

was watching me carefully however and—so, on second thoughts I took my notebook out of my pocket, placed the page carefully inside it, then took a stab at it:

"*Deutsch*—well, that means German—something German..."

"Something German..." he says, imitating, me sarcastically.

"It's like the name of a registered company..." I says. A travel company maybe, or a travel agency..."

He scoffed.

"Aye, sure!" he says. A travel agency, indeed!

Chapter 6

He took a few sips of his drink in silence as if gathering his thoughts and suppressing his irritation at the same time, then spoke as follows:

"It's rare that people see what's in their best interest.

And it's the business of the police to keep the public on the right track, particularly when they don't realize where that track lies."

"That's when they should get a small rap of the stick, surely?"

"It is of course!" As the old saying goes. "If you stitch some-one with a blow, make sure you stitch them twice."

"I knew a young fellow myself and he got seven stitches in the head that way one time!

Says he:

"Let me never kill anyone,
Let no one ever kill me,
But if anyone is killed
Let it be me that kills him!"

"As I often say, many's the man who doesn't realize what's good for him. You often get people on the run from us who'd be far off far better off if they'd been arrested by us. This Irish-language Erfurt whom you say you don't know at all—if he's on the run from us in Ireland, it's probably just as well for him—even it's a stupid move on his part. His situation would be far worse if he left Ireland because the Irish Gardaí Síochána are like tame house poodles in comparison to the wild, hungry mountain wolves that are Interpol.

Come on! Come on! Someone involved with the Irish language movement and Interpol are on his tail! Come on! No one would believe that! The Irish authorities barely recognize the existence of the Irish language and here's you telling me that a top-secret international police force are interested in someone who's involved in Irish language affairs. I can't take something like that seriously!

He gave me a sharp look, and said:

"I hope you're not as innocent as you look my friend. Many governments throughout the world have always been apprehensive about Irish. And why wouldn't they be? A European Union (if one accepts that the island of Ireland is part of Europe) and it their sworn duty to promote a language that's still alive despite the best efforts of our government to destroy it over the past 100 years!) Isn't that a major worry in itself? If Dr Hyde and his band of merry men had succeeded in their attempts to revive the Irish language across the nation back then, wouldn't this country be governed by smugglers and con artists and bootleggers and gangsters and chancers of every description? And all of them speaking a language that was saved from its demise by crooks and fugitives and desperados of all types. Sheep-stealers and cattle-rustlers, brigands and highwaymen of every description. Thanks be to God that a different type altogether had been attracted into that new movement—a fact that saved the movement even if it didn't save the language. But it was out of the frying pan into the fire in reality! Because the next major threat that emerged from the Irish Language Movement was the fact that her ranks were filled with patriots and trade unionists and republicans and socialists and collectivists and communists and all the rest of it. Luckily, the government of the day responded promptly to this huge threat—(thanks be to God we had our own government in place at the time)—and laws were passed to ensure that the Irish language was taught in every school in the country and that it was compulsory for the Garda Síochána and civil servants. This saved the country from the second major threat posed by the Irish language. Because, by making Irish compulsory, they generated a hatred of the language in every part of the country and particularly amongst the younger generation."

"I find your views very interesting Sergeant but I don't see any connection between this and the man Interpol are on the hunt for!"

"This here is the third major national crisis that the Irish language has precipitated! That there are people from outside the state now trying to infiltrate the Irish language movement!"

"Who are they?" Or where are they from?"

"A rough and dangerous crowd, a strange group of lawless thugs and hooligans eager to cause trouble and chaos over here! Europeans and Ulster people! Immigrants and the Ulster crowd! Yanks and Ulster-heads! Hippies and Mods and Rockers and Ulster-heads?"

"A lot of the Ulster crowd so?"

"They're everywhere these days?"

"And you don't like them, is it?"

"I'd like them more," he said, "if the whole lot of them were brought out into the middle of a lake together on a boat and they sank it straight away!"

Chapter 7

There was no point in me telling him that there were no
Ulster people involved in things at all, as far as I knew—
but anyway… I couldn't admit to knowing too much about the
Irish Language Movement and its activists however.

"I'm sorry but I don't I still don't see how a Gaeilgeoir could
be in trouble with the police, no matter what he got up to, particularly with Interpol! It must be very serious if they're inves-
tigating it."

It is very serious as Interpol don't get involved in something
unless it's got an international dimension to it!"

"But, sure, the Irish language isn't international!"

"It wasn't prior to this but, because of this new gang, this
Erfurt von Volcano individual—the likes of whom has inter-
nationalized a movement that was confined solely to our own
small green, little country previous to this—the language has
assumed an international dimension now. Moreover, the
global powers and the international companies are increasingly
concerned about the Irish language once more. Our nation's
ancient language currently poses a threat throughout the entire
world."

"For God's sake Sergeant, what has this Erfurt fellow done
that's so out of the way?

"It's a long story but the first fraud he was involved in related
to the grant of five pounds a year that our government gives

to the Irish-speaking families of the nation. There's nothing international about this, of course, but he expanded his scam in a fiendishly clever way so that the five pounds was available to people outside Ireland. He's been teaching Irish underhandedly to people all over the world so that they could get the £5 pound grant, even to people living in areas that classed as the Third World. As you can imagine, given the levels of poverty in those countries, he was hoping to make a huge amount of money from this scam."

"I see" I says. "Of course! Of course!" The people in those parts of the world are so poor that you could buy a Fianna Lay from them for the price of a bowl of oatmeal!"

"Exactly! We know what he was charging in the Republic of Chad, for example. Three verses of newly-composed poetry for the price of two potatoes! They got the same money for one-and-a-half potatoes in the Upper Volta except that their standard of Irish wasn't high enough."

My head was in a spin! The potential for such a scam was shocking. Take a very poor country such as Bangladesh, for example. For a bag of flour, a half-dozen turnips, a barrel of porter and a box of tomatoes, you'd possibly have got the *Foras Feasa ar Éirinn* and accompanying music as provided by a choir of 300 people! Surely, the government and trade officials would be driven mad with jealousy and rage at the likes of this.

"Bad enough" I says. "It looks like this guy's up to his knees in it now though, the poor idiot!"

"If he'd had friends who were true and honest, they might have set him on the right path. But if Interpol get their hands on him!"

"From what you've told me so far, Sergeant," I says ignoring what he was getting at, "it seems to me that the poor devil was doing good things for the sake of the Irish language the whole time anyway?"

'Are you joking me?' the Sergeant said lifting the bottle off the table to make sure there wasn't a drop left in it.

'If he'd focused solely on Irish language issues, he'd have been fine and Interpol wouldn't have been so interested in him. That wasn't enough for him however. He wanted to turn the whole world upside down! If he'd just stuck to Irish and bothered with languages like Morngin and Baining and Uvea!"

"I don't know what you're saying here Sergeant, to be honest, but I still find it hard to fault a man who was trying to revive the Irish language!"

"Amn't I'm telling you that he was trying to revive Vogul and Tabasaran and Hadzapi as well as Irish."

"I don't know who Vogul and Tabasaran are…"

"They're not people, but languages, for God's sake!"

"Yeah, but I still can't but admire someone who's main focus is to save our language from the death that threatens her."

"Don't try to diminish what this same gangster was up to! Because there was nothing limited or small-scale about his plotting and scamming. He claimed to be trying to save 500 languages which are still spoken, the majority of which are threatened with extinction."

"I didn't know that."

"I didn't know it either," says Sergeant MacContrary, "until I was researching this case and got to know a little bit about some of these minority languages in the process. The likes of Kru and Igbo. In the heel of the hunt, I became quite fond of such languages generally and began to collect them in much the same way as people collect dried herbs, or butterflies or seashells.

Chapter 8

Some people say that the police can be hard-hearted and uncaring. That said, it's often the case that their hearts are in the right place. Beneath the blue uniform with the harp-shaped buttons frequently beats a generous or kind heart. And the same goes for many's the detective also. And who'd believe me if I was to tell them that this big tough-looking man folded his arms across one another on the table, bowed his head and cried his eyes out. And the cause of his grief was the five hundred languages that are dying in five hundred different places throughout the world.

I says:

"This man that you're hunting for—he must be very well-disposed towards languages also…

The detective admitted as much, wiping the tears from his eyes…

I used to know very little about languages and I couldn't have cared less whether they survived or not to be honest—until very recently—and I became very concerned about their welfare. Do you know what it's like..? It's like falling in love… That's how it feels…

"It's worse than that still if you look at it more closely…for the individual who's agonizing about the fate of all of the languages…" It's like the case of the old woman who lived in the shoe and who had so many children that she didn't know what to do. Given that a policeman ought to be to be seen as tough and strong—both mentally and physically—there's always something particularly moving about one of them who demonstrates they're a softie or very sensitive underneath it all."

I says:

"The struggle for survival of the Irish language—that's enough for me any day of the week."

"There are many other languages in danger of death in addition to Irish!" he said.

"But the human race is in danger of extinction also," I says, in an attempt to raise his spirits somewhat.

"Arah—feck them anyways," he screeches. "It's the languages that I'm stressed about."

He fell silent for a few minutes and I realized that the best thing for it was to let him empty himself of all his pain and emotion by talking to someone else about it. I was sorry that all the whiskey was gone but there was nothing I could do about that. He told me then how the whole thing had got such a grip on his imagination the first day ever.

"I saw this tragic programme on the television about the languages that are only spoken by..." he says, snivelling and taking a hanky out of his pocket... a few hundred people now."

"The poor languages!" I says.

"How awful they must feel in a situation like that?"

There was a catch in his voice when the Sergeant spoke next.

"There are two languages spoken inside the Arctic Circle."

"They're probably frozen, the poor things." I says.

"They've been trying to do the same to Irish for years—put it in the freezer is what they want to do it with it all the time!"

MacContrary blew his nose.

"The same languages are inside the Soviet Union too!"

"The poor creatures!"

MacContrary had his back was to me at this point—letting on that he was looking out the window.

"I hear that the Soviets are trying to keep these languages alive. Printing some of Marx' and Lenin's works into these languages in the Cyrillic script and that kind of thing—is what they're at."

"Are they really?" I says, suppressing a sigh.

"As if the poor languages haven't enough to be worried about, as it is!"

"They shouldn't do that! You'd have thought the Russians—more than any other crowd—would be colder and more ruthless in such matters. They should just eliminate the poor languages and put them out of their misery, shouldn't they?"

I began to weep myself now too just thinking about it.

"Isn't there somewhere in the southern part of the Soviet Union, in a region between two inland tidal areas where each individual village has its own language?"

This news horrified MacContrary so much that his weeping stopped for a moment.

"That's terrible altogether! How could you enforce any rules and regulations under such circumstances?"

"I don't know," I says. "I'd imagine that any policeman based in such areas must have a right dog's life altogether—if he didn't agree with the community on every single statute and rule."

It wasn't long before we were both in tears again just at the thought of all the languages worldwide that were on the verge of death.

"I never really understood until now," says the Sergeant just how lonely a form of communication or a language must feel in the knowledge that its community is abandoning it forever. A language the likes of Odissa say…" <u>Odia? 35 million</u>

"Or Tulu, for example!" <u>1.85 million</u>

"Or Fang!" <u>1 million</u>

"Yao!" <u>3.1 million</u>

"Nicobarese!" <u>30,000</u>

"Efik!" <u>400,000</u>

"Cree!" <u>96,000</u>

"Hopi!" <u>7,000</u>

"It'd break your heart just thinking about them!"

"Would you drink a pint?"

"I wouldn't say no to one."

We dried our eyes and went down that eight flight of stairs arm-in-arm. That bout of weeping had done the world of good for us.

Chapter 9

I dreamt that night about the sudden arrival and departure of the armed rebel women from foreign parts. The incident had been as a mysterious and bizarre link between this world and the next, so strange and bizarre that no one would ever have believed us if we'd told them about it. The sergeant and I researched the subject and tried to find out about similar-type incidents but we turned up very little information.

Brendan O'Worried had an uncle whom they said had a lot of information on the history of the movement to revive the Irish language and so we went to him to see could we learn more on the subject. He had many stories about the various scams and scandals associated with the revival but—even after he'd finished telling us everything—his insights didn't relate to our concerns a great deal.

"Did you ever hear of the Little Priests' Revolt?" says he.

Needless to say, we'd never heard anything at all about it.

"It happened in the early 30s when the Association of Gaelic Priests was in existence and some of the blame probably lies with them in the first place. Because they said straight-out that the Catholic Hierarchy were not giving as much support to the Irish Language Revival as they should have been. This was a strong statement to make at the time and when the bishops didn't take the slightest notice of it, the Association felt that words were no longer useful and that swift action within the
154

church was required—something along the same lines as the revolution against the state of both Pearse and Connolly.

So, some of the novice priests took over the best-fortified buildings in Maynooth University. It goes without saying that they had the hierarchy in a tight spot—initially at least. In the end however, it turned out—as is typical of Ireland compared to most other countries—that the older generation emerged victorious over the younger people. The government backed Maynooth in the stand-off—sure, what else would they do?

And the media backed the older crowd as well ensuring that not a whisper or a word about the situation reached anyone outside the gates of the University. In this way, the College authorities managed to keep everything secret from the Irish public."

"Once the news black-out was in place, they arranged a cease-fire and peace talks to weaken the rebels' position further and derail them from their initial objectives. They promised to elevate the status of the Irish language immediately and forgave the organizers of the revolt for their actions. They played on the religiosity and natural idealism of the trainee seminarian-rebels until the latter promised—for fear that the chapel and the library might suffer any damage—to leave the buildings they'd occupied, locations they'd selected as the best from a military strategy point of view. Little did the trainee priests know then that a full battalion of battle-hardened men from the ranks of the Christian Brothers was awaiting orders just outside the gates of the college as well as a battalion of the Mercy Sisters. The latter group had joined with the Fire Brigade and were ready to attack with an array of water cannon and they'd an unlimited seven-day water supply at their disposal. (The Irish Jesuit Order initially offered some minor weaponry to the rebels but the Papal Nuncio vetoed their use.)"

Once all the terms of the cease-fire were put in place and the Little Priests' forces were barricaded or trapped between the kitchens and the dormitories, there was a sudden change of tune amongst the spokespeople for the hierarchy and the college authorities however. They gave up trying to change the young men's minds and get them on side and began threatening them instead. A fight ensued but it didn't last very long once the nuns had turned the water cannon on them and the rebels' courage soon dissipated. In went the Christian Brothers then with the hurleys and various small batons and they lashing all around them as the students retreated from room to room. It's not clear what happened to the clerical students once they'd surrendered but it is said that some of those who emerged unscathed were sent to China on the Missions afterwards.

Now, there is no reference to this dispute in any of the history books, nor in any other book as far as I am aware. No documents exist anywhere recording that an incident such as this ever happened. And when I asked Brendan O'Worried's uncle if he knew of anyone who could confirm the truth of these events, he admitted that he didn't—a fact that leaves me dubious about his entire story ever since.

He had another story that was interesting also, whether true or not. It concerned a priest from the west of Ireland who had spent his entire life as a missionary in Africa, and whatever happened to him—whether he began losing his faith or losing his mind—what do you think he did but instead of teaching religion to the poor pagans, he began teaching them Irish instead.

The local tribe had always had great respect for him since he first came to live amongst them. Therefore, between the Christians who listened to the Gospel from him to keep him happy and the pagans who refused to listen to him in case they disagreed with him, everyone still loved him. Moreover, when he began teaching Irish instead of the faith both groups were happy to attend his classes and the Mass House was always full to the door.

This situation continued for quite a long time as there were few of the new developments in modes of travel or in theological matters that there are today. In fact, it would have continued like this forever if it wasn't for an article in the *National Geographic* magazine written by an engineer from Edinburgh who claimed that some of the African languages were related to Scots Gaelic. His view was derided by linguists in every quarter who wrote very sarcastic and demeaning letters about his theory to the newspapers but the writer in question retorted that he could prove his claims.

This was how reports of this elderly overly-Gaelic priest living in remotest Africa who'd abandoned his duties to the faith gradually reached the authorities in the Vatican. The millwheels of the Church grind slowly however and a fine newly-ordained priest was assigned to replace the elderly priest who was transferred to a small Presbyterian island off the coast of Scotland.

As mentioned earlier, though, it's impossible to be certain whether the stories related by Brendan O'Worried's mother's brother were entirely true.

Chapter 10

The elderly Gail who was a member of the Goethe Association proved more than happy to help me with my enquiries.

"A huge fellow altogether! That's Erfurt von Volcaniceruption without a shadow of a doubt! Don't ever annoy him for God's sake, whatever you do! Ha! Ha! Ha! He's one of the biggest men I've ever seen in my life! Well over six foot he is! He must be nearly seven foot, I'm sure of it. And the same girth and width nearly, the same man!

He's a good man! I know well where he lives but I wouldn't know the number of his house or his exact address. Do you know the Baroness? Her house is on Kilmacud Road and the Big Man lives near her.

This was very useful information. An extremely tall man—it wouldn't be too difficult to locate him if he was still in the area. The Baroness could tell me where he was too even if I only wanted to call on her as a last resort.

It didn't take me long to find the right street whatever about the right house number. I walked up and down outside the house but no go; there wasn't sight nor sound of him. I'd just have to hang around there for a while, I decided. So, I spent the guts of the next three days at this crack and just as daylight was beginning to fade on the third day, I spotted a huge man emerge from one of the tall, dark houses, scan the streets carefully and then walk swiftly down the path on his side of the road. I was standing in the shadows of the trees on other side of the street when he appeared and so I crossed the road and hurried after him. This was a very stupid thing for me to do and I wasn't long paying for my stupidity either.

In fact, that payment nearly settled all my accounts forever! Following a man the likes of him was as crazy a thing as anyone has ever done.

He left the street behind and escaped down a lane that ran behind the houses. From there he rushed ahead, crossed the street and disappeared left down another lane. And this was where he waited and attacked me! Whether I'd a sudden premonition or not but at the very last second, as I turned into the shadows in after him, he swung a deadly blow at me and I backed away just in time. I didn't escape his follow-up however—those big hands of his -they were like the shovels on a giant digger. I went down but jumped up again immediately, coiling my body like a fish in a net to escape him. Like a flash, he was on top of me. I squirmed and twisted but I couldn't shake him off; I felt his hot breath on my neck. There weren't many people around -- just an old woman in her garden across the way, looking on. He gave a jump and managed to grab hold of my shirt and coat and we crashed to the ground.

We were wrestling viciously on the ground and I gave a muffled scream: "What're you doing! Trying to kill me, is it!"

And in a deadly voice, that is exactly what the big man confirmed—he was intent on throttling me. I was terrified in case he managed to get those two giant hands of his around my throat when the old woman across the way started shouting:

"This is no place for fighting and thuggery. Where are the Guards? You should go into the middle of town if you want to kill one another." We continued to the death-struggle, the pair of us grappling and wrestling on the hard ground.

"Hey! That's not a fair fight! No way! That giant is way too big for the small fellow," the old woman called. There was no one around to hear and in the end, you'll never believe what saved me. You'll never believe it—it was the cheap shirt I was wearing!

If I'd been wearing a quality, homespun Irish-made shirt, I'd have been finished! Instead, when von Erfurt let go of my coat for a second in an effort to grab me by the shirt-collar with his two shovel-hands, didn't half of the shirt come off in his right fist! Next, he tried to wrap the damn cloth around my head to choke me but the shirt tore again and I managed to squirm out of the way. "Hey! Hey!" says the old woman watching us. "They're tearing the clothes off one another now!"

The shirt ripped again and I was completely free of him and running like the wind—I left him left standing there in the road with bits of that imported third-grade stuff flapping in his hands.

Chapter 11

I sprinted as fast as I could go even if I knew—without looking around—that he wasn't far behind. Where could I go
to escape him? Where else but the one house that I recognized—the Baroness' place! This was how the pair of us ended
up bursting through the main door into the big hall of her
house—one man hot on the heels of the other—without so
much as a preamble or warning—frightening the life out of the
poor woman!

The Baroness came flying out of the sitting room and stared
at us, eyes wide with shock. She opened her mouth as if to say
something but nothing came out, she was so stunned, then
ushered us quickly into another room. The back door opened
and who should appear through it but Sorley himself and he
gawping in astonishment!

The Baroness had turned white in the face, alarmed as she
was at the sight of two men barging right into her house—one
man raging with bloodlust and the other blood-spattered and
half-naked. It was a spectacle that would have frightened most
normal woman. But then, she was no ordinary women—this
same Baroness—and it was difficult to work out who she was
more angry with—me or the Big Man. She cross-examined von
Volcaniceruption first, then brought Sorley out of the room as
well to discuss the matter with him privately. I sat there quietly

without a budge out of me—like a prisoner banged up in the well of the court awaiting sentence.

"Ok, everything's decided," says the Baroness when she came back in.

"You'll stay here with us as we want you to take part in our great attempt at levitation come next Spring. You're not a prisoner here technically but you won't go anywhere without von Volcaniceruption going with you. And you won't be inclined to go anywhere much either because you'll be too tired from all the work here. Because these trials we're about to begin are very different from the amateurish, half-serious efforts we ran prior to this. Up to now, we didn't take the project too seriously as we were only gathering a very small group of people together and working out what issues and difficulties were involved. Along with the others who're partaking in this great attempt of ours at levitation, you'll become so accustomed to the Lotus Position that after a while you won't choose any other way of sitting down. The reason for this is that there's no better sitting position for the human body, from the point of view of comfort and nature—once you become used to it. By becoming accustomed to such a sitting position, you will be able you to focus your attention completely on the levitation aspect of the project. And dedication towards our goal isn't enough of itself; it is group dedication and focus as achieved by a small number of people working in unison that's required. If you have need of in-depth meditation and discussion at any point, all arguments or disagreements will be avoided—as we are all physically and psychologically focused on the one communal objective and goal."

What else could I do but accept her instructions and diktats?

I said to myself that I'd stay with them and help out around the house, in addition to demonstrating dedication to the cause and the various practices they were trialling and testing. It would be as if I were in an open prison. Or in a monastery of sorts for men and women with the Baroness as Mother-Abbess.

Sooner or later, I thought I might get a chance to escape. I didn't however. I soon discovered that escape wouldn't be easy. I wasn't long realizing that this was no open prison or convent either. I was a more like a prisoner on death row instead, someone who'd already received their death sentence as well as the time and place for execution!

Von Volcaniceruption explained the whole process to me in detail. He followed me everywhere I went—right down to when I went to bed at night. I was assigned a small bedroom at the top of the house—one with bars on the windows! And my bed was right across from his—the bed that took his enormous weight. He kept the key to the bedroom and to all the doors of the house on a chain around his neck and he'd regularly explain to me in a very calm manner all the different ways that someone could be executed or put to death!

Chapter 12

As a teenager in the Luftlandtruppen was where he'd gotten his training in the executions, during the Second World War. I told him that if they were thinking of killing me—then, they wouldn't get away with the likes of that in Ireland. But he told me that there would be no difficulty whatsoever about getting rid of me! In fact, they'd already decided that if this levitation trial we were preparing for didn't work out, I would be thrown over the edge of a cliff nearby! Von Volcaniceruption would go down to the bottom of the cliff—in an attempt to save me, supposedly—after I'd been thrown over the edge—but, in reality, to make sure that I was definitely dead. Then Sorley and the Baroness would call the guards to inform them of my death.

It was dawning on me now that I'd been taken prisoner by a group of nut cases who were quite happy to eliminate me if I didn't come through this crazy trial of theirs safely. If we didn't succeed in achieving the impossible, they were telling me, I was finished; my time on this earth was over. The big man following my everywhere was quite similar to the prison guard whose business it is to monitor the condemned person's every step. And from the way von Volcaniceruption spoke, I knew that he'd have been quite happy to wipe me from the face of the earth at any stage, if the Baroness gave him the order to do so! As regards the Baroness, the more important thing in the

world was that the next levitation trial or test proved successful. Except that the Baroness had a hunch that I was the weak
link in the chain that was the mystical train of hope in the Irish
language—required for all of us to levitate. She had good reason for this hunch of hers also. But because it could be read on
my face, despite my best efforts, that I just couldn't take this
talk about people raising themselves off the ground by the
power of the mind and their strength of will seriously. Fair play
to Sorley who was happy still to speak up in my defence. Having said that, I was disappointed to see that he didn't reject this
stupidity about levitation more. In fact, instead of rejecting all
this craziness, he promised the Baroness that he'd make sure
my percentage of Irish language diligence and hope was at a
high enough level to reach the required stage of fanaticism
required for levitation.

It was the Baroness herself who'd have the last word and
who'd decide my fate.

In truth, she'd already made her decision—this test would be
a trial of me really. If they succeeded in levitating from the
ground, there would be no stopping me from living to a good
age and dying in my stirrups. It still bothered me a lot that Sorley couldn't see his way to doing anything else—except trying
to build up my faith in this craziness. As the Great Levitation
attempt drew closer and the days grew longer, the tension only
increased between me and the other three. So much so that
Sorley rounded on me one day:

"It appears that you're not really as devoted to the Irish language as you should be," he says.

And then the Baroness says:

In the history of this country, many's the person who suffered
a terrible death as a consequence of how devoted they were to
the Irish language. It's rare enough to see people who're in the
situation that you find yourself in now—whereby the greater

your belief in the Irish language is the one thing that will save you!

My mind was in a daze—trapped as I was between the pair of them! And no matter what, I had no intention of accepting even one of their allegations or accusations. Sorley again:

"Despite it all, you still don't have the look of someone who believes in the revival of the Irish language."

He shook his head and gave me a despairing look while von Volcaniceruption just looked from one of us to the next—like the hound that's been promised a bone.

I thought to myself that the best thing I could do was to keep them guessing—neither be truthful nor dishonest with them. As long as they didn't fully understand me, I had some chance of emerging unscathed from this death-trap.

Chapter 13

"The first book in Irish that I ever laid hands on included an Introduction in English," I told them.

"An Introduction in English?" says the Baroness and I could tell by her tone that she was sick of my story before I'd even begun it.

"Yes, an Introduction. And it included a warning regarding Irish in the Introduction also" I says, feeling slightly emboldened at the look of disgust that clouded her face; the same when I saw the negative and suspicious glances I received from both von Volcaniceruption and Sorley

According to this tutorial book, there were issues relating to the Irish language that are *peculiar to the Keltic languages.* That book that left me suspicious and distrustful of the Irish language ever since. For all I knew, studying this language might do permanent damage to my senses. It might affect me like a drug for all I knew? Like LSD say? For all I knew, it might leave me confused or disoriented in a psychological or physic sense? I could easily see how the strange grammar of this language might leave the scholar's personality lenited to the day of their death. And all of their endeavors and work on other schemes and projects could be left constantly aspirated and people inflicting urú's on them day on day. For all I knew there might be something disguised in the language that couldn't be sensed and that might leave me damaged for the rest of my life?

"Still and all," says the Baroness sardonically, "I don't get the feeling that learning Irish affected the sharpness of your senses in any way. And I doubt that it did any permanent damage to your cuteness or slyness when it comes to plotting or planning either? Do you mean some kind of psychological problem? Do you think that some kind of disorder might reveal itself in your personality?

Are you trying to blame the language of this country for the psychopathic traits in yourself?"

I ignored these questions and took a different tack however.

"It's true for you that I mastered the Irish language but no sooner had I succeeded in that particular battle, another problem revealed itself—one equally as worrying to me. I had completed my studies in Gaeilge (Irish), the language. Now it was time for me to study the Gaeilgeoir or Irish-speaker. I followed Irish-speakers around. I listened to them. I observed them. I got to know them and I the same places they did."

But I had nothing at all for all my troubles! I still had no proper understanding of the Irish language movement and it seemed to me that I never would. Whoever understood the roots and meaning of the Irish language movement... they'd have understood the meaning of life itself. They'd have sourced the mystery of being and eternity. And I'd have been quite happy to have left it at that too—only that Sorley and yourself lured me into taking part in this great experiment of yours."

It was on the tip of my tongue to say: *The defence rests* in that moment—but I didn't bother.

Maybe everything I said wasn't entirely true but this was still a good summary of my viewpoint. After all—take any man trying to protect himself from the death penalty—it's has always been accepted that such a man has the right to bend the truth slightly to save his own skin. And even if what I said had disgusted von Volcaniceruption and annoyed Sorley, I sensed that for the first time, the Baroness realized that I was someone with a complex and sophisticated mind of their own.

This was major progress really seeing as she'd always regarded me previously as some odd and incomprehensible being—a member of a species that had come from another planet. She turned from me however and addressed a different question to the others.

"We've never succeeded in recruiting new members to our movement previous to this. At the end of the day, the only real disciples I have are the two of you and this buck here (pointing in my direction). The others who come to this house can be divided into three types:

Number one: the hungry crowd who call in here to eat my sauerkraut and white pudding. Number two: the homeless people who come here looking for a place to sleep even if they claim that they come here to practice the lotus position and to examine their navels! The third type who call here come for the sake of the Irish language in much the same way as the first crowd call for the white sausages and the second crowd to snore and fart inside in the parlour. If they aren't really sufficiently serious about levitation for the sake of the Irish language, they're of no use to me! I felt sorry for her. She wasn't looking for my opinion on the subject but I thought I'd give it anyway.

Everyone knows how quiet and gentle and respectable a crowd the ordinary members of the Irish Language Movement are and there's no point in relying on such people for bizarre or unusual activities the likes of this levitation project. In addition, there's no organization in the world no matter how respectable and civilized that doesn't have a fringe group who are half-crazy and yet travel the same road. The Noisy Wing, the Illogical Wing, the Wild-eyed Wing, the Crazy Gang. They're in every organization and they're on the fringes of the Irish Language Movement too!

Chapter 14

A nd she listened to me on this occasion also! Von Volcaniceruption was sent out to capture the Foreign Professor, Whiny Maolchú and Brendan O'Worried and imprison
them by use of force—the same as they'd locked me up. It
didn't prove easy to force the Lotus Position on Whiny
Maolchú, even if Brendan O'Worried was a different story (as
he was able to take comfort in the physical pain involved!)
Whiny Maolchú was a long time giving me daggers from
between his knobbly knees before he submitted to the trial
even if the Foreign Professor was no trouble at all. Wasn't this
what he'd always wanted? To have time to bend and twist his
own body into the same form as the Egyptian Water Lily.[8]
You'd have thought it'd be some improvement on my situation
that three of my colleagues had been captured as well as me,
and over time, I got a chance to explain the situation to the
others one by one. Not that this was worth my trouble! I soon
realized that instead of dealing with three crazies as I had been
prior to this, I was now dealing with six of them! All I heard
from Brendan O'Worried that it is in the nature of the Irish
and the Gaels to endure torment and suffering. One day I got
a chance to tell the whole story to Whiny Maolchú who
thought about it for a while and then said:

"What's wrong with the Irish Language Movement is…"

8   Sacred Blue Lily of the Nile

I ran away from him as quickly as possible.

Strangely enough, the Foreign Professor was the only one amongst them who give me a bit of support. At least, he gave me something else to focus on. I listened to him say:

"The majority of people believe that summer birds migrate abroad in order to see the other side of the world—in the same way that tourists go on their holidays to foreign parts. The reason birds migrate is in search of food and in the hope of finding enough to survive on, every bird in accordance with its own needs. A species is essentially a living form that's found a way or another to sustain itself and grabbed the opportunity enthusiastically."

Chapter 15

The Foreign Professor fell silent. I didn't say anything as I could see he was bothered about something.

"Could you imagine a seabird living to the same age as the same age as a human being? Such a bird in the finest of health and still breeding away at 53 years of age? There is evidence of the existence of such creatures as based on an extended study undertaken at a nesting site of the albatross of the species *Laysan* where more than 13,000 of them were examined over time! You'd imagine that a bird as large and powerful as the albatross would be capable of a great deal but the evidence gathered indicated that the percentage of them that breed from year to year varies. Where you'll have 100% of the birds of breeding age producing offspring one year, you might have only 40% of birds of a similar age breeding in a different year again. Scientists worldwide are currently researching this issue."

"This is likely a source of concern to them" I says.

"Additional information collected by them as part of the same study indicates that more than half of the birds over fifteen years of age are still breeding and a third of them aged twenty or more continue breeding. Seabirds normally live longer than land birds anyway. Even the smallest bird amongst them, one that's only the size of a swallow *Hydrobates pelagicus*, or the storm petrel (*Peadarín na Stoirme* or "Little Peter of the

Storm" as our forebears called him—they had so many different names for him in the Irish, demonstrating just how fond
our ancestors were of this small bird). If this bird is lucky, it
will live without aging too badly until it's at least twenty years
of age and it doesn't even consider breeding or settling down
until it's four or five years old. So why wouldn't it have
longevity? Moreover, if even if there are big differences
between the two aforementioned birds with one being the
smallest of seabirds and the other the largest—they are actually
related to one another far out, believe it or not!

There are eleven species of albatross that belong to the same
genus. If you added another two special species of albatross to
the equation, they form a family group all their own and can
be assigned to the Procellariformes Order."

And three other family groups exist alongside them, one of
which is the storm petrel that dives regularly, the other comprising the petrels as related to the sparrow; this third group
comprises sweet Little Peter, the Storm Petrel."

"There you go now with the four family groups that make up
the Procellariformes Order; the meaning of this Latin term is
that they are generally quite sharp, bill-hooked creatures. This
trait of theirs means that they are able to judge the direction
of the wind and they are very good at sensing changes in atmosphere and weather. Another important trait of theirs is the
shape of their stomach. Their stomach-glands are bigger than
those of other birds and signs on it too! This highlights another
incredible trait of theirs, the supply of oil they have on-board
at all times. This is the case with every bird of the Procellariformes. And this is actually the meaning behind another name
as ascribed to the bird known as 'Little Peter' to the Tory
islanders—i.e. the 'Gearr Úisc', translating as 'small bird filled
with oil'. (The islanders used to get the oil for their lamps from
the cadavers of such seabirds at one time.)"

"These two seabirds—the albatross and the petrel—differ from one another in many aspects also. When the largest of them—the albatross—begins its courtship ritual, the male bird and his first love perform a dance that is more complex in its movements than either *The Siege of Ennis*, the *Humours of Bandon* or the *Eight-hand Reel*. Not only does the female take an active part in this dance but other birds looking on also join in. The dance itself involves the raising and lowering of the wings, the stretching of the beak into the air, the slapping of feet on the ground, and sideways movements of the head. Of course, it's easy for an enormous bird the likes of this for whom travelling long distances is a regular aspect of life—to organize a céilí out on an island cliff-edge!

A much smaller bird, the storm petrel, prefers a different form of social life and enjoys nothing better than spending the day skimming across the waves and breakers until sundown. And come nightfall, it prudently and warily returns to where it makes its home—a hole that looks more like a rabbit burrow than it does a bird's nest! Similar to the rabbit, the petrel gives a quick rap on the door to get in home, and the same for every member of the species in that colony. On arrival, they go their own way, like tenants in a big block of flats! The smaller creatures of this world need to keep on friendly terms with others and the Little Petrel is so small that some of his neighbours might be tempted to look at him with hungry eyes! The Great Black-Backed Gull, the Great Arctic Skua, or the Gannet even."

Any one of them could gobble him down and they'd still be hungry afterwards. He'd make a nice snack, oil and all!

You'd think maybe—seeing as they're related far out—that the albatross might cease its constant, boring circling and show solidarity towards a much smaller bird?" You'd think that the Procellariformes might stand shoulder to shoulder in solidarity with one another!"

"That's not how life works however. If birds gave in to nostalgia and romanticism, their life would be as chaotic for them as it is for human beings."

"The fact that they're related to each another is recognized nonetheless even in the way each of these birds gathers its food. Maybe our ancestors referred to the smaller bird as "Little Peter" in honour of Saint Peter in the Gospels who walked on water until he lost courage? Probably. Because this small bird makes a movement that's halfway between walking and flying, its spindly, little legs astride and its wings fluttering, thereby enabling its continuous skimming along the surface of the tide, collecting plankton and all the many other tiny forms of sustenance that live on the top of the waves."

"One needs skill, durability and endless patience to gather one's food in such a tedious and tiring way. You'd wonder that the albatross hasn't come up with a better technique for foraging in order to sustain itself. The latter is reliant on its ability to travel long distances and in the knowledge that it'll have a stroke of luck at some stage. Patiently waiting for that which comes along only rarely—that which proves well worth the wait. It is normal for such a bird to be make do with the leftovers of a much larger feasts, whichever of the spoils slipped through the clutches of some greedy gut or other.

It's incredible the range of sustenance the sea provides and yet it's amazing how far away from one another the places where this wealth of food is located. It is incredible how long the barren stretches of water between each food supply can be also."

The Foreign Professor finished speaking. I didn't say anything myself. And even if he hadn't provided any advice or support in relation to what potential fate might await me, I felt slightly better after his lecture all the same. Even if he evinced no interest whatsoever in my troubles or predicament, just listening to him had raised my spirits and done me some good.

175

Reflecting on the trials and troubles of the feathered brigade rather than my own. My situation was bad enough but in a strange sort of a way, by reflecting on the struggles and sufferings of these poor birds I felt consoled somehow.

Chapter 16

Finally, the big day came around when we set out through the hills and mountains following behind the Baroness in a line. We were in good shape physically and mentally following the non-stop trials we'd undergone in the Big House out in Kilmacud so climbing up into the mountains didn't knock a stir out of us—as we followed this amazing woman uphill through the wilderness of ferns and bushes. Eventually, we reached a circular-shaped sand pit on the mountainside at the centre of which lay a tunnel. As we made our way over to this pit, I could see that the earth in this area had been disturbed. The entrance to this pit was draped with a series of plastic sheets and camouflaged with bushes and foliage, behind which something was hidden. We stripped away all the branches, grass and other foliage to reveal a bright, aluminium disc that was seven feet high and twelve feet wide.

"It's a flying saucer!" says the Foreign Professor.

We opened the door of the saucer and entered it hesitantly one by one.

"But where's the engine in this?" says Whiny Maolchú.

Because the interior of the flying saucer comprised bare and shiny aluminium, the same as the exterior but inside, the spacecraft was completely empty. Next thing, the Baroness instructed us to sit down on the floor inside and form a circle, each of us with their back to the bright, circular walls of the machine. She asked us to assume the Lotus Position, each person equidistant from the next; we'd to focus our thoughts in unison and begin the deep meditation that we were all well used to by then.

The Baroness von Wink addressed us as follows:

"In truth, such entities as space or length or width do not exist. Within every human heart is a small chamber containing sky and earth and fire—air, sun, moon, stars and thunder. We are properly balanced whenever the pressure on the exterior equals the stress or tension within. It is the people who embody this state of constant balance that are the ones…"

We should not assign too much importance to the contours of this inner chamber; neither should we allow the pressure outside to worry us or make us anxious. It is not that we should ignore such matters or

remain deliberately unaware of them but rather that we should agonize over them no more. The two forces or pressures—inside and out—should begin to cancel one another out now. As our beings begin spinning with the saucer as one, our souls will be bathed in unity and oneness… let us synchronize our thoughts and focus on our primary objective…

It's as if we see the light of a ship far away on a dark, starless and moonless night—the mysterious powers of the personality are in the ascendant now. Instinct and hunches have replaced reason and the border between the realms of body and soul is penetrated. There's a good chance that we'll fall into a daze now or lose consciousness. I ask you now to let yourselves go and to sink perfectly into the ripple-free pool of peace and calm.

Chapter 17

My head exploded with a powerful light and I felt the saucer rise into the air. There was no doubt about it— we were moving. It swayed initially and then began to spin at speed; next thing, it rose up high in a straight line at incredible speed! It was as if we were in an elevator that had whirled out of control and spinning towards the gates of heaven, to meet Saint Peter. My earthly body felt as if it was plunging to earth— soul and senses departing for a more glorious plane—a planet that was paradise.

And when I recovered again, the pounding pain in my head and the hammering in my ears was gone and replaced by a new feeling. I felt as if I was swimming through a waterless atmosphere, a place that became colder from moment to moment.

"Where are we? What's happening to us?" was the question on everyone's lips. "Why's it so cold?"

The calm voice of the Mighty Woman herself came to us and it was as if she was our schoolteacher again back in the old schoolhouse in County Leitrim.

"We're 30,000 feet above sea-level now, crossing the Atlantic Ocean. And from now on, we're beginning our descent; we're on a trajectory that will bring us halfway across the world to South America."

"Is that good?"

"If our coordinates are correct and we're on the right trajectory, we'll land in the highest-located body of water in the world, Lake Titicaca, smack in the middle of the western mountain ranges of that continent. That won't be too bad."

"And what happens if we're not on-course properly?"

"The saucer will turn sideways."

"It'll turn sideways!"

It was clear that she hadn't given this possibility a great deal of thought prior to me asking the question! After all the effort, she'd put in making sure that we rose from the ground—up into the air from the earth that'd given life to us—it was clear that she hadn't paid any attention to this aspect of our project prior to this.

"The saucer will move sideways. If our altitude is very high, we'll pass over all of the mountain ranges in the Pacific region. If we're too low, we'll land in the upper regions of the Amazon River amongst those wild tribes that hate all white people; this is the place where their favourite hobby is making sure that strangers suffer a long, slow and painful death. There's a good chance that our flight-course means we'll land somewhere that's in between each of those possibilities. That's what we're hoping for—that remain on a steady course and land somewhere in-between—that we fly neither too high nor too low and maintain a balance in-between at all times.

Says I to myself:

"Isn't this how things should always be? In-between forever, similar to the average standard of Modern Irish students today."

"I glanced in the direction of Whiny Maolchú—now was the perfect time for him to tell us what was wrong with the Irish Language Movement; or to tell our Woman-Leader what was wrong with it—in order to keep this Irish-language project of ours on the correct course—right up through the heavenly skies—so that Irish would live on as one coherent entity—

rather than being shattered into smithereens forever—along with ourselves!

"There is also another possibility!" she says then, in a strangely hesitant tone of voice and we waited for her to speak.

"Another possibility that we didn't pay a great deal of attention to. That we could go too high or too low and be smashed into a million tiny pieces if we crash into the face of one of the roughest mountain ranges in the world.

Everyone fell silent at this chilling possibility.

But after a few moments of deathly quiet, I says to myself—Sure there's no harm in asking another question anyway.

"So what's keeping us airborne right now? How come we don't plummet straight down into the ocean as we speak?"

"Haven't I just told you?" she says. "We've now begun our descent back towards the earth, in a gradual fall."

"If we were moving in the opposite direction now, the movement of the earth's axis would ensure we were carried halfway around the world. But just after take-off, we found yourselves high above Ireland with a strong north-east tailwind behind us and this blew us out over the ocean while we were still ascending—so that we are now on-course for the west coast of South America."

"But how did we take off in the first place?"

"Do you not get it? It was our mutual love for the Irish language that ensured we had the power for take-off! Our common hope and conviction in the future development and growth of the language—this is what gave us the power to rise up into the air in the first place!"

Whiny Maolchú didn't look one bit happy about this. It was obvious from his face that he felt the Irish language had inflicted a monumental injustice on us—the way it had dragged us halfway across the world and left us powerless to land at a destination of our choosing—somewhere where we knew we'd be balanced, safe and secure.

Chapter 18

That's the real down-side of having high ideals and noble aspirations. When held communally, they can ensure you levitate or get off the ground but you've no control over where you go once you are in the air! Whatever way you we look at it—whether moving up, down or just floating on the air—the process of ascending or descending from the ground is a directionless one. Once you've risen straight off the ground, the question that immediately raised itself was—what direction do we go in now? There is a choice to be made at this point, a judgment involved... it's a different intellectual process entirely!

Sorley said that we were as well to keep going seeing as the Baroness "had brought us this far already." Supporting the motion, Brendon O'Worried said that he was quite anxious about the situation we now found ourselves in.

"Don't tell me that we're in trouble?" I says.

It was obvious that we were though... we were up to our necks in it.

"Even the smartest people make mistakes" says von Volcanoeruption.

"Those of us who are of German stock have the reputation that we research everything and trial it carefully with the best information available to us before we attempt any new project or initiative. And yet, despite this, have to admit that our best efforts aren't always enough. Not that this absolves us in any way from our duty to try our best in every instance. Even if in certain cases—as has happened here—that our best efforts to undertake this mission safely have been destroyed, squished and blasted into smithereens against the high walls of these rock-solid mountains here—into which we are going to crash at any moment now!"

"How did it all go so badly wrong?" asked Whiny Maolchú. "What exactly is the problem here?"

And the Baroness responded:

The issue here is that the highest mountains in the world—barring the Himalayas—are in our way. That's the crux of the matter."

"But didn't you say that those mountains were between Lake Titicaca and the Pacific Ocean?"

"I did and they are! But they're also standing high between the lake and where we're flying right now…"

Despite everything, she was the schoolmistress to the very end.

"The Spaniards associated these mountain ranges with two giant chains stretching across both sides of the sea known as Lake or Sea Titicaca and they call this mountain range between Lake Titicaca and the Pacific Sea 'La Cordillera Occidental.' The mountain range we're in danger of being smashing to pieces against—they call this 'La Cordillera Oriental'."

She couldn't help exhibiting a bit of masterly female humour at our predicament:

"Not that our demise will bother people too much."

"God help us and save us as," I says to myself, even if I'd never been particularly well-known for my religiosity or prayer. The words just slipped out of me, I was that terrified at the prospect of abruptly exiting this world.

"What other ranges are as high as 'Cordillera Oriental' says the Foreign Professor. "Sorata Ilamu and Illimani, they're two mountain peaks that are between 21,000 and 22,000 feet high."

"Now, that is high!"

"It sure is. If you made Carrauntoohil three times higher and stuck it in the middle of Lake Titicaca—a lake that is itself located 12,500 feet above Pacific Ocean or sea-level, it would reach the same height as the Cordillera Oriental. Also, on the Cordillera Oriental—between the Pacific Coast and the banks of Titicaca you find mountain peaks that are just 1000 feet off the height of Sorata Illampu and Illimani."

"And where are we likely to land? If God grants that we even make it!"

I couldn't help myself. Alive or dead, I was always a curious buck!

"Lake Titicaca lies in the Altiplano! That's where they'll tell stories about us some day! It's the sheer height of the mountains on both sides of us that's the most frightening thing right now."

"What's our altitude now exactly," I says. The baroness had an altimeter on her.

"We're at 13,000 feet and falling."

Suddenly, Brendan O'Worried gave a roar out him, something that he never did, and we stared across at him, afraid he might have lost it. Next thing, however, he burst out laughing, something else that he rarely did either.

"No problem!" O'Worried suddenly says. "No problem at all! Oh ye of little faith! I have it! I've the answer," and "There's only one way for us to get out of this. We all have to muster our communal courage and will it to its apex again so that we can get over the Cordillera Oriental at its highest point. But immediately again, we need to suffuse our hearts in despair and sadness with respect to the Irish language cause and everything relating to it and this will bring us into a swift and safe descent into the waters of Lake Titicaca."

"There'd be no harm," says von Wink—sharp, prescient and astute woman that she is—she took Whiny's words on-board—

there'd be no harm in us raising our communal hopes and emotions as regards the survival of Irish once we're halfway down—a swift and sudden upsurge in our aspirations regarding the revival of the language right at the midpoint of our descent—in case we hit the lake-water too hard."

"Definitely, I says, "We don't want to drown straight away."

"That isn't it exactly," says the Baroness. The fact that we're lacking exact data and we don't know just how deep the water is in Lake Titicaca is—that's the problem. If the water's not deep enough to soften our landing, then we might hit the water so hard that we'd end up smashing right down into the floor of the lake before we know it."

"We'd be crushed to bits!" says Whiny Maolchú.

"That's certainly a possibility that we can't ignore," says the noblewoman, and reverting to her schoolmistress tone of voice.

Now, I don't need to remind you how important it is that we stick to our flight-plan. Firstly, we need to raise our communal hopes and emotions in tandem so that we can make it over the top of the mountain range and then an immediate and sudden collapse in our hopes for the future of the language to ensure a swift descent in altitude—then, right on time, a last-minute surge in our hopes and aspirations for the revival of Irish just before we hit the surface of the lake. Everyone's up to speed on the plan now, aren't they?"

Sorley and von Volcaniceruption gave her plan the thumbs-up.

"Seeing as our communal hope and belief in the Irish language has brought us this far—and our aspirations for its revival—there's nothing surer than that this same combined hope will ensure we emerge from this crisis safely also."

And would you believe it, dear reader, if I tell you that everything went exactly according to this plan also?

It sure did. And within ten minutes we'd landed and were trying to stay afloat in the waters of the highest lake in the world.

Well let's be precise in these matters—the inland waterway that was the highest above sea level anywhere in the world. I won't claim that we were in any real danger of drowning at any stage but it did take all of our efforts to bring the flying saucer and all the rest of it ashore. By which time a small handful of local indigenous people had appeared on the shore to watch them. Even if I live to be a hundred years old, I'll never forget my first sight of these exotic people. They all had the same appearance—both men and women—or so it seemed to me anyway. Nut-brown skin and raven-coloured hair, long and flowing. Hard bowler-shaped hats jammed tightly down over the eyes and ponchos or shawls in geometric shapes circling their shoulders, dark-black skirts worn to the feet. A series of dead-set stares from inscrutable and emotionless faces—it was impossible to know what they thought of us—whether hatred, anger or just plain curiosity! They looked on as we wrestled the big aluminium saucer to the shore of the lake. I can't remember now what was said except that one of our group—Whiny Maolchú, probably—spoke to the local people in a rude and rough way.

Not that his words had the slightest effect on any of the people looking on. Except for one person. I'm not sure who he was—who left the others and approached us:

"Are you here for the Irish language? Follow me until I show you the way up to the College!"

"Donegal Irish! I couldn't believe my ears! I still don't!"

Chapter 19

We followed this man and were delighted when he introduced us to the officers of the Deutsch-Keltische-Stiller-
Ozean-Genossen, those people from central Europe who'd
worked in unison to transplant the Irish language on a commercial basis across some of the most remote areas of South
America. The members of the group were delighted to respond
to our questions about this amazing region we'd just landed in.

I mentioned the similarities in appearance amongst the people we met on the shore of the lake—and we were provided
with two different explanations for this. It is a particularly
European trait—or so the anthropologists say—that the men
grow facial hair. Amongst many tribes in the Americas and in
the Pacific Ocean and Asia, men and women's faces are quite
similar from a facial hair point of view however.

The second explanation we heard related to a drug. A drug
that stood to the people of these regions through hardships and
oppression in the same way as poteen stood to the Irish under
similarly difficult circumstances. If you were to ask a group of
these people who were worn-out and who'd suffered a great
deal of hardship after travelling for weeks through the roughest
of mountain terrain with little in the way of food—if you were
to ask them what kept them going, the response would be a
simple one—Coca!

It is always on the back of the misery and suffering of the poorest of the poor—that the richest build their wealth and sophistication. And those classes of people deemed most sophisticated and urbane of all in the modern world—have always had a huge reliance on the most inventive forms of this same drug. And the true story of this drug belongs to the long-suffering, dead-pan and worn-out faces that we met on the banks of Lake Titicaca that day.

But the issue that was really bothering the likes of Brendan O'Worried, Whiny Maolchú and myself—the one that'd left us chewing the nails off ourselves to try and understand—how was it that foreign peoples such as the Germans, the Danes, the English, the Austrians, and God knows which other national-ities—how had they all made such a good fist of a problem that'd tormented, worn out, and exhausted people in Ireland for so many years?

Even if they hadn't five cubic centimetres of Irish blood between the lot of them—there they are trying to save our national language, despite us! And the most excruciating part of the story is that they are succeeding also! In addition to the Irish language speakers of the Altiplano, they're now boasting at least two other thriving Gaeltachts on that side of the world now! One of them is an island on the west coast known as la Isla Maldita. Another one is in the depths of the rainforest, the Latachúnga Gaeltacht. And all of this going on unknown to the Gaelic League! They've put us to shame completely!

The three of us agreed right there and then we had a subject of protest here. That we needed to make a complaint about this. It was obvious that there was something unjust about this whole thing, even if we weren't too sure where exactly the injustice lay or what exactly was wrong about it. But the ques-tion we asked ourselves was: Are we happy to let foreigners away with this? No way! Not a chance! But seeing as there's a right way of setting about things and a wrong way, we decided

to set up a committee to investigate the situation. In the meantime, we asked the locals the controversial question straight
out:

What gives you lot any right to work in the Irish-language
field in the first place? And what gives you the right to do successful work in this field either? And whatever the story, tell us
what skills you have in this area that have been denied us, the
Irish of Gaelic stock, for hundreds of years now?"

Von Rumata was the name of the German whom we ques-
tioned about these issues. As regards our first question however, he was initially as reluctant and unforthcoming as any
Irish TD or public official would be in such circumstances!
That said, he didn't mind sharing his insight into the successful
techniques utilised by this Germanic Gaeltacht-foundation of
theirs.

It's incredibly simple and easy to explain," he says. And the
system works a treat also. What we do is examine very carefully
every strategy the Irish government and Irish-language orga-
nizations implement in relation to the revival of the language—
and then we do the exact opposite to what they do in every
instance. Since we first adopted this formula and strategy, we've
been going from strength to strength. Our approach has never
failed us yet!

Chapter 20

All right—there's no doubt but that it was difficult to ignore the effectiveness of the work they'd undertaken. They are an amazing people, the Germans, no question about it. When you see them at work, you'd think that nothing in this life is impossible to them. Growing potatoes to sustain an entire population appears one and the same to them as growing potatoes just to eat them. They don't perceive any difference between both. Maybe they are right also as what do human beings require from their environment but the same thing that plants require? Shelter—that's to say sustenance, protection and preservation—that and additionally, the potential to grow and develop. The right to drink the dew when it's free to drink. It is just a question of freedom—the escape from restrictions, meddling and deliberate negativity.

How often in Ireland had I listened to the language brigade talk of planting a seed? Or the fruits of their work for the language cause coming to bloom—that was another one! And about ploughing on… and all the rest of it. The endless speeches concerning branches and supports and things coming into bloom. How given they were to metaphors taken from the sowing and reaping and the life of the land. Even if the vast majority of the language activists were scholars and academics—tidy, clean people who'd never dirtied their hands picking potatoes or bringing home the harvest.

But as for these here Germans! They'd had made a complete ass of all our poetic metaphors regarding the revival and rebirth of the Irish language! Because the way they saw it—founding a new Gaeltacht was as easy as planting a field of cabbage. They'd made right fools of us! And if someone didn't put a stop to them, they'd have Gaeltachts and half-Gaeltachts sprouting up in foreign parts before we knew it!

"The Latachúnga Gaeltacht is in Ecuador and it's no small or easy journey to get there either. It'll take you something between a week and 10 days to get there and that's using the most reliable modes of transport available too!"

This was how representatives of the Deutsch-Keltische-Stiller-Ozean-Genossen spoke concerning the journey that lay ahead of us and they weren't exaggerating or making things up either.

The attitude and approach of these German Irish-language activists wasn't that easy to work out either. There was nothing Irish or Gaelic about it, that's for sure. There's a big difference between "Irish-language work" and *"Arbeit Gemeinschaft un zu Irischsprach Bewarrunge"*.

This might have been one hell of a mouthful to say but its implications were more overwhelmingly still! If these Germans were let away with things, would they soon fill remote areas everywhere with small Irish-speaking Pleasure Gardens?

They needed to understand that there's never been paradise or pleasure garden anywhere that didn't have its own jealous snake slithering around inside it. And they'd been in contact with me already. An agent from *Las Naciones Disunidos*. I don't know how they worked out that I was the weakest link in the chain of the *Deutsch-Keltische-Stiller-Ozean-Genossen*? But it was me that one of their agents approached anyway—one day when I was in the city of La Paz.

Von Rumata used a jeep for business in the surrounding towns Arica, Arequipo, Puno, Huancane and one day, I was sitting in the front seat waiting for von Rumata who was in the *Banco Minero de Bolivia* when a very well-dressed stranger approached me. That was the beginning of it.

Needless to say, his business had nothing whatsoever to do with the Latchúnga Gaeltacht which we were then preparing to set out for. He was focused on that other island, a place he'd had his eyes on for a long time prior to that. That golden-island Gaeltacht of ours over which the sun sets out in the Pacific Ocean—la Isla Maldita!

The place they wanted to test out their bombs in!

Chapter 21

We took a coach the following day along the main road from La Paz to Lima, to the airport there. I've often heard people complaining about bad roads in Ireland (where some of the best roads anywhere in the world are to be found!) All I can say is that what I experienced on that trip cross-country will stay with me for as long as I live. From La Paz down to Lima, the road passes through areas with mountains and cliffs more frightening than anything anyone has ever seen. It was the length of Ireland—from Malin to Kinsale three times over, that's how long this wild journey lasted, just imagine that?

And the company that provide the bus refutes the notion that any bus driver has the right to take a break or have a rest at any stage between La Paz and Bogota. They don't put up with any excuses whatsoever from the driver who breaks this rule. "The only excuse is death," they say, "and that in itself is a poor excuse!"

If you take this bus then, you're accepting that you have to fly along at a crazy speed on a crazy road in the company of a crazy driver. The bus company who provide this service boast of how many atheists and great sinners fall to their knees in intense prayer during the course of this incredibly dangerous and incredibly crazy journey.

And if you reach Lima safely, another long trip of a similar kind awaits you. The same if you reach Quito. It's just as well that there are airports in both cities. Airports are a huge asset in regions that are so wild and remote. The travel companies that kept these services in the air were something else too. A half-dozen, battered old aircraft that had been repainted, re-modelled and re-built, piece by piece, most of which were war-planes recycled from World War 1 and 2 and other lesser-known conflicts. Anything that shortens the journey in a coun-try with such incredibly-long distances between one place and the next, is to be commended. And many's the traveller who jumps for joy at the sight of such a plane when they know what a torrid journey awaits them in the absence of roads to certain areas. And if there was always a small chance that a traveller's life proved briefer than normal, it's also true that half of the people who took this danger upon themselves survived all the same. The passengers who boarded those airplanes were happy customers and they were seven times happier again when their feet touched the ground again on arrival.

The third section of the journey was the worst in that it involves hardship as well as all the dangers relating to a tropical forest in a mountainous country.

At this stage, four-legged animals such as horses, mules and the species native to that region—the Llama—are essential to travel, even if the latter isn't very fond of the thick woods and forests.

These hardy animals can make their way along the harshest of routes but there are some trails that even these animals require the help of human beings to navigate, and that's the reality of the situation. Up till now, no-one has considered it possible to convert an ape into a beast of burden, or to make a pack animal out of a monkey!

Unsurprisingly, there was no little preparation required for such a journey. It necessitated more than just packing the right equipment. A certain degree of training was also necessary to achieve optimal health and physical fitness so that we were ready for the last stage of our journey to the Latachúnga Gaeltacht.

Chapter 22

That said, everything went as planned for a finish. Other than one bizarre incident that occurred as relating to the Foreign Professor. It was his own fault, needless to say, as he kept separating from us the closer we got to Latachúnga on our journey west. Of course, it was his crazy obsession with birds that was behind what happened. The objective of our journey was to act as peace envoys in that area as there was a real danger of a major dispute erupting between a mining company that was operating in this area and our Gaeltacht people there. We'd been warned beforehand that it was a very dangerous area and that we could be fired upon by the forces of the Latachúnga Women's Army; the latter were very upset about the whole thing, especially since the mining company had threatened the government on them. The Deutsch-Keltische-Stiller-Ozean-Genossen favoured that all sides held their fire for the moment. And they certainly didn't want anyone on the government payroll being shot as such an incident would really fan the flames in what was a very volatile situation already.

We failed completely to persuade the Foreign Professor that there was any danger for him in this situation however and he actually left our group before we realized he was gone at all! He left with just basic provisions in his knapsack and a pair of binoculars swinging from his neck, ready for use the minute he spotted any birds. It never occurred to him that there might

196

be other pairs of eyes watching him all the while with great interest and an insatiable curiosity. It was these binoculars that caused all the trouble and it was a bad job that we didn't confiscate them from him the first day ever. The further we travelled on that arduous journey through incredibly-thick forest and jungle from Quito west past Cotopaxi and onto Chimboroso, the worse the Professor became. This was when he started waffling on about some bird that the experts weren't sure whether it even existed or not or whether it had become extinct. *Vagabundus vagabundus* was the name of this bird and the Foreign Professor constantly went on and on about it while he wandered around—all day long, oblivious to anything that didn't have feathers. He was in a world all his own—the world of birds. If we hadn't been keeping an eye on him, I think he probably would've tried to take off and fly at some stage. By then, we were all worried about him and it wasn't easy— between the incredible heat and the sudden change of climate as well as the shock to the system we'd experienced on plummeting into Lake Titicaca—we were all worried that the poor man had lost his mind.

When he claimed that it was close to the Latachúnga Gaeltacht that he'd have the best chance of spotting this lost bird of his—it put the kaibosh on the whole thing completely. "*Vagabundus vagabundus* indeed," I says! "There would have to be something unworldly, poetic, exotic about such a creature—given that it inhabited a place where Irish was spoken! What else!"

Anyway, we were just three days away from our final destination when the Foreign Professor disappeared on us. We were struggling at the time to make our way through a wilderness of jungle on one side of a mountain when the professor went missing. The rest of us can't be held responsible for the mess he got into at this point; it was his own fault entirely! As usual, the Foreign Professor had completed most of the journey as well as any of the rest of us—or even better than some of us, in fact. Some people say that the devil takes care of his own while others say that the Almighty protects the fool—and you can make your own minds up about the Foreign Professor in this regard.

As regards the wild Gaelic women of Latachúnga, they spotted him coming a mile off. It was easy for a group of them to follow him on their hunkers and to surround him even, he was so completely oblivious to them, obsessed as he was with the birds. In fact, a group of them followed him around for an entire day keeping a close eye on him and trying to figure out what he was up to. People say that they stole all of the Professor's possessions from him and he never even noticed—then gave them all back to him again having examined everything carefully—and that he remained oblivious all the while. Whatever about this, I don't believe something else that I was told about the female freedom fighters—i.e. that they allegedly stole a half-written manuscript in Irish from him, made corrections to it, and then gave it back to him again—without him ever realizing that it had been missing in the first place. I wouldn't put it past them all the same! That's the type of thing that they were experts at.

They found it very difficult to make any sense of the Professor however—never mind what he was up to!

"What's really bugging me…" says the female leader of the group assigned responsibility for spying on the Foreign Professor and reporting back on him—"What's really bugging me is trying to make out what the hell this joker is looking at all the time through those damned double lens of his."

"We should just shoot him right now and be done with it!" says one young woman, stretched out on the ground as they rested for a few minutes. "Isn't it obvious that he's a spy? Isn't it obvious that those twin glasses of his are spy-glasses of some description, isn't it!"

"But what's he spying on? That's the question."

"He's letting on that he's surveying the terrain around here" the same young woman says, "but he's actually trying to spy on us really! For sure—he's spying on us so's he can get in with us and become one of our crew!" But their leader shook her head.

"We'd have eliminated him immediately if he was carrying a listening or spying device of some form. There's no way we'd let him away with trying to listen in on our conversations. But as he's definitely using some kind of a looking device, we need to find out what he's looking at. It'd be silly for us to kill him before we found out what he's looking at. "What's he doing now?" says another messenger who'd just arrived in? "He's staring up into the sky, right into the sun," says the Young Gunwoman. The leader of the women's militia's eyes grew wide with wonder.

"He'll get blinded by the sun as well as sunstroke the way he's going on."

"I've a really good cure for sunstroke!" says the Young Gunwoman, shaking her rifle. "If you'd only give me the chance!"

Chapter 23

The leader ignored the trigger-happy gunwoman and continued assessing the situation. For the previous two days, the woods around about had been alive with armed rebel women coming and going—all of them keeping an eye on this strange visitor of theirs. Despite hours of chat and discussion however, none of the women were too sure why exactly this individual with the binoculars had appeared in their area. Was he a mining surveyor? And the binoculars on him surveying here, there and everywhere? Was he a botanist searching for a rare form of tree or plant—some strange form of meadowsweet that grows in the fields or some type of agrimony? Was he a military man? Or a deserter maybe? But a trained soldier would have had enough sense to keep himself as close to the ground as possible; he wouldn't have been wandering around openly in a strange area with binoculars swinging and over and back from his neck. Maybe he was some sort of an official appointed to one of these "mickey-mouse" government jobs they'd heard about recently—some poor fool who'd been released from some military academy or other... maybe that was it...

A spy of some description... maybe that was it? Spies went into new territories and surveyed them for the others that followed on later, didn't they? The leader of a group of scouts spoke:

"God give us strength! If we only knew what's so fascinating that he spends all day, every day, peering through those binoculars of his. "You have to admit that he is not a very good spy! if that's what he is. A spy who lost his way in the jungle!"

"He'll be lost for good if you give me a shot at him!"

"It's in their nature for young people to be impatient at the best of times."

Their leader was thinking aloud. "A spy who's lost? Well, he's definitely gone in the head if he thinks he can wander through our area here and get away with it!"

"I'd give my right arm," she says, to know what he sees through those special spyglasses of his."

"Whatever it is, he's fixated on something at this very moment," says the younger woman. "He's been staring out at the water on Lake Rapids now for a good while—whatever's out there."

"And what's he looking at now, for God sake? They've every new-fangled device on the go these days, don't they?" says the trigger-happy Young Gunwoman.

"Is it that he's getting some sort of a message or signal from someone or somewhere we can't see?"

"How do you mean?"

"I don't know. Maybe some sort of a radar or holograph or something—I'm not sure…"

"We need to get those special glasses or lens—or whatever you call them off him—so that we can have a look for ourselves."

Chapter 24

The Foreign Professor never saw it coming. He didn't know what happened to him; one minute he was enjoying his most favourite hobby in the world and the next he'd been forced face-down in the muck and a powerfully-built woman had pinned him to the ground. The binoculars were torn roughly from his hands, the strap knocking his glasses off.

He hurt his nose in the altercation.

The woman who swiped the binoculars off him was now peering through them:

"I can't see anything except lake-water and the odd bird here and there, that's all!" she says.

"There must be something there," says the boss. "Look again!"

"Here" Have a look yourself so!" the younger woman says, passing the binoculars over to her.

"You're right. There's nothing there only birds and water. I don't get it…"

"Maybe he's just looking at the birds?"

"For what?"

"I don't know why but the old crowd who lived here before the arrival of the Irish language used to say that you could make sense of the world around us based on how the birds behaved."

"That's just old superstition!"

"Maybe. But maybe this fellow here is superstitious for all we know?"

"Well, say now that he's been employed by a mining company. That crowd would cosy up to anyone get one over on us. The boss was quiet for a moment before giving her take on it:

"We've to watch this lake around the clock until we work out what's going on here exactly. In the meantime, keep an eye on this fellow girls," she says, giving the Foreign Professor a kick for good measure before leaving to present their findings before a council comprising the eldest women in the community. By the time she'd return to the clearing where he was trapped face-down in the mud beneath the weight of his burly captor, her group of fighters had worked out what the Professor's business was doing there—and they'd worked it out in their own way also.

The minute she'd left, the entire group of women fighters surrounded the Professor and began to rough him up a bit. Between them, they weren't too long getting the truth out of him

The Young Gunwoman was the one who kicked off things:

"Now man, spill the beans! We know you understand Irish and this indicates that you're spying on us. Tell us more."

The Professor's voice, when he spoke, was weak and difficult to understand:

The burly woman grabbed the Professor by the hair and pulled his head up so that he that they could hear him better. "Now, we know that you can speak Irish," she says, giving his head a bit of a shake.

"*Vagabundus vagabundus*," he says and the women looked at each other.

"That's not Irish," she says, giving his hair another pull.

"That's the Latin word for it," says the Foreign Professor.

"The Latin word for what?"

"The local people around here would have a different name for it maybe, I can't remember."

"Well, you better remember it quickly!"

She gave his head another shake.

"Hang on! I remember now! It's the wandering landrail."

"What?" the gun-woman says, her face screwed up in confusion.

"It's the name of a bird."

"The name of a bird! What does it mean?"

"Vagabundus vagabundus. This is the only place in the world where this species is still found…"

"Listen here Mystery Man!" the eldest woman in the group exclaimed. "You choose your words carefully now and explain it better, will you? What's this about a bird's name? And what brings you to these parts? Take your time now or it'll be worse for you, believe me…"

The woman holding the Foreign Professor down shifted her weight off him slightly to make it easier for him to respond.

"Vagabundus vagabundus. The wandering landrail. Or the wandering corncrake. Whichever you prefer. This is the only habitat in the world where it can still be found. It's nearly extinct at this stage."

"Get to the point man and explain yourself to our satisfaction or you won't be long going extinct yourself!"

"The wandering landrail! It's a bird!" the Foreign Professor said with a screech.

It's unclear how thing would've ended up if one of the more senior women in the group hadn't piped up that she'd heard tell of the wandering landrail previously. That was enough to save the Professor's skin for the time being—even if some of the other women fighters stil had their doubts about him!

"Everyone keep their eyes glued to the surface of that lake!" the woman who'd swiped the binoculars insisted, unable to disguise her suspicions. The burly woman who'd been holding

204

him down had to admit that there was something very romantic about the idea that a man would go out into the wildest of jungle terrain and rainforest in search of a bird that was nearly extinct. Her fascination with this man whom they'd squashed into the mud was further piqued.

"What can you see now love?" says the eldest of the fighters to the woman with the binoculars. "What's that you're spotting on the surface of the lake across the way?" The woman with the binoculars didn't respond immediately but when she did, there was a quiver of emotion in her voice.

"I've often heard it said that this world is going crazy but up till now, I assumed this referred to the people only. Now, I can see that even the birds of the air are going crazy on us now! O Mother! Tell us what all this means? Is it the really end of the world?"

"If this isn't it," she says, "the end of the world isn't far off anyway, that's for sure!"

The fighters got a fright on hearing this and gathered more closely around the woman with the binoculars

"It's incredible, really incredible. What a display!" The two birds draw close to one another as they rise up chest-first out of the water and puff out their breasts. They stretch their necks in the air and then give a series of savage thrusts into the water with their beaks—after which one bird resumes circling the surface of the lake while the other submerges itself once more, its head breaking the surface every few minutes.

"Foreign fellow, it seems that you are a man of some knowledge when it comes to these lake-water birds…"

But the Professor paid her little attention—he was too interested in finding out whether there was a second species of bird visible on the lake.

"I can see now…" she says, peering through the binoculars, "two other birds there too and in answer to your question—

all I can say is that they appear to be dancing on top of the water."

"What's wrong love? What is it for God's sake?"

"All I'm seeing now—even if my eyes can barely credit it—is a big huge bird skimming across the surface of the lake and an enormous spout of water streaming down either side of it. This giant flying creature half-swimming, half-floating over the lake, wings extended -it's making great wide semi-circles on the surface of the water!

Chapter 25

The Foreign Professor tried to sit up, he was so excited. "That's all?" he says, even as a heavy thigh jammed him face-down into the mud again.

Undeterred, he wiped the muck from his beard and asked again:

"That's all ? Isn't there a second bird there?"

Another fighter gave the Professor a dig in the ribs.

The woman with the binoculars lowered them and gave him a cold stare.

"Hey, foreign guy, whoever you are—maybe I've seen enough now!"

There was no stopping the Professor, now that he'd returned to the only subject he'd ever expressed an interest in—and his muffled voice came up to them out of the muck:

"The second bird is usually under the surface of the water but she pops her head up and reveals herself from time to time…"

She raised the binoculars to her eyes to check this out and a moment later:

"It's true for you Foreign Fellow. You're right about that!"

This information made some of the other women anxious however and one of them said:

"Put down those glasses now love! Maybe we shouldn't assist this foreigner with whatever strange magic he's involved in!

The binoculars woman ignored this comment however and continued with her commentary:

"This is incredible really—absolutely incredible!"

The pair of them are dancing on the surface of the water the same as you'd see two people dancing in the dancehall of any local town!

"Are they dancing together or are they adopting different parts in the dance?" the Foreign Professor asked excitedly.

"Well, right now, one of the birds is busy dancing while the other is looking on and watching the display. The one who's performing raises his head, pulls it back and puffs out his chest, then dives down into the water. When he rises again, his appearance is amazing. It's as if he isn't a bird any longer but some sort of ghostlike creature instead—given the way he twists and turns his shoulders and his neck. He dives beneath the water repeatedly before emerging each time with this strange look or shape about him. Both birds go off dancing together like two people at the end of which, they turn their backs to one another and swim away in opposite directions!"

"That's incredible altogether!" says the Professor.

"But what does it mean?" all the women fighters said in unison.

"The most amazing thing about it is to see birds from the northern hemisphere this far south! It's not that certain birds don't travel this down this far past the centre circle—it's just that here in South America they have their own unique species of birds. The two species of bird that you saw there—you, the woman with my binoculars—I wouldn't ever expect to see them down in this region normally—the Ghostly Penguin Dance is what the experts call this unique dance of theirs through my binoculars. This species of bird is known as the *Podicepsauritis* or the Russian Grebe! It rarely visits these parts.

Those of you who saw it are really lucky. But the large bird you saw skimming along the top of the water—people call that the Loma or the Luma—others again call it the Great Northern Diver. The experts who use Latin to describe the birds of the sky refer to it as the *Gavia immer*. That imitation of a speedboat that you saw him performing earlier—that's his normal method of courtship!

In that moment, the fighters realized that this man they'd captured wasn't just any foreign English-speaking intruder who was up to mischief and they let him up from the ground. He was neither a treacherous spy nor a dangerous intruder— but rather a fine specimen of Irish manhood who'd travelled from the city to promote the development and expansion of the Gaeltacht and its community and to protect them from whatever group might try to oppress them.

Chapter 26:
Conclusion

The wealthy don't understand the poor is what they say. If only that was the sole issue! Men don't understand women. It often happens that parents don't understand their children and vice-versa. In truth, the whole world is a constant conflict or struggle between different types of understandings. Employers don't understand their workers nor workers their employers. Customers don't understand the difficulties of their suppliers and nor do shopkeepers understand the complaints of their customers—and neither do the readers of novels understand the pain and suffering the writer goes through trying to produce a novel or even a fable itself for them. A person who's writing a book can be compared to a pregnant woman—except that they can't be excused in the same way as the person who's lacking in organization and energy—someone who can be forgetful, irregular and erratic in everyday matters. The statistics show that Ireland is full of people who began to write a book but who didn't stick with it or complete it—what's the person with the half-written work of literature like? They are like someone with a dangerous cyst growing on their skin that sucks the energy and life out of them.

We need a special metaphor to describe the typical Irish-language writer with their half-finished novel. The Irish-language writer who's been working on their novel for years can be compared to the "old-school" farmer who wants to see his head-strong daughter—(who shows no inclination to marry even if the this is the heart's desire of the old-fashioned farmer)—settled down and secure for life, before he himself goes beneath the ground forever. Similarly, the poor, old Irish-language writer seeks nothing more for their novel than that it finds a secure and permanent publisher or home.

Given that I myself have been remiss in the conception of this novel, it is my duty to see it through to the end. To ensure that it's maidenly title finds a proud home next to a publisher of high-repute, the pair of them standing together in ornate lettering, whether in softcover or hardcover, in the capable hands of a dutiful bookbinder that recognizes the solemnity of the occasion.

Right now however, the worst part of the story (the worst part of the novel?) is that which holds me back—the fact that I can't work out whether a tragic or grief-filled ending or one a happy and joy-filled one is the most appropriate conclusion to my story.

This story of mine isn't such a bad one.

She bears no animosity towards any reader amongst you. I would like her to be happy. But I would also like her to be innocent, pure of heart, and as truthful a history as possible, particularly given the corrupt times that we live in. The difficulty I am left with is that I have to arrange things so that a certain joy is woven into the truth—and it is rare that these characteristics merge as one. To resolve this quandary, I've decided that this novel should have two conclusions in order that the reader can choose their favourite ending.

Dear Readers!

I'll leave it up to yourselves decide which type of conclusion you'd prefer to have to your novel in Irish. You can have the choice of two endings as a conclusion to this story.

These days, there's a lot of talk about equality amongst people. I challenge any writer to acknowledge that the reader who enjoys reading a book through damp eyes and tears has as much right to read a book as the reader who gives a load roar of laughter at the beginning and end of every page they read.

From now on (wait'll you see!) no reading public anywhere will be satisfied with the author who finishes their story but doesn't provide the choice of two endings for it. As for myself, I'd like to be remembered as a pioneer in literary matters. The first Irish language writer who sought to give value for money to the readers of novels in Irish. Henceforth, every novel will have two conclusions...

This is a major development and yet, you can never keep everyone happy. For example, the overly-dutiful and deeply-logical group will always be with us! And one of them will speak out as follows:

"Two endings to a story! That's impossible, isn't it? There can't be two endings to one story—no more than there can be one dog with two tails?" Well, I admit that this is the way most people think usually—that this is the *norm*. That something has to be either one way or the other, either true or false. That two contradictions cannot exist simultaneously.

Chapter 27

A nd this was how I viewed life myself—until I first got to know Doctor Don'tmindit, that is.

He was an unusually clever man Doctor Don'tmindit- no doubt about it? Who would he have reminded you of? Well— Looks-wise, he was very like Boris Karloff or his like, as you'd see in the old horror films—but whatever about that, you should know that I am greatly obliged to Doctor Don'tmindit! In fact, I don't know where I'd be now without him to tell you the truth! Locked up somewhere probably. Either that or in a straightjacket in one of the psychiatric hospitals.

When I returned to Ireland from South America, I was rotten with money. I reeked of it. And prior to this, I never thought that someone with money could have difficulties or problems. But *I* had a problem myself—a problem of conscience. I went on the drink even if I drank alone most of the time. I avoided other people, the Irish-language crowd especially. What could I say to them if they began to question me about Whiny and the Foreign Professor and Sorley and the Baroness von Wink?

I was reared in the same faith as the majority of people on this island. Unsurprisingly therefore, I thought of going to the priest to tell him about my problem. I could've told Father Givingout what was bothering me, for example. A big man for the Irish language I remember him giving the speech at the Feis one year—so I thought about him. But it was just a fleeting thought…

"Oh Father!"

"Well there, sonny my boy, have you done anything bad since the last time you came to Confession?"

"I destroyed a Gaeltacht."

"I couldn't hear you there. Speak up young lad! Don't be one bit afraid in God's presence…"

"Good Father, I took part in the complete destruction and elimination of a pure Gaeltacht area—between men, women and children—(particularly women!)…"

"What could he say? Besides his question and my reply, I couldn't think of what else to do. Other than escaping that confession box. Out of the church and Father Givingout roaring loudly behind me…

I could've gone to the local bishop or to the Pope in Rome but I didn't. To Dr Don'tmindit is who I went to instead…

He's from the Middle East originally and he came to Ireland to undertake a study on us. I remember an interview with him published in one of the newspapers. I liked his views a lot.

"The Irish person worries far too much about the harm they've done in the past instead of being worried—as any normal person should be—with how much harm someone can do to themselves."

"This man's the lad for me," I says to myself. Here's someone who's on our side rather than always knocking us. He mightn't improve Ireland as a country but he'll definitely improve me. So I arranged to go and see him immediately. I knew well that it costs a lot of money to consult the likes of him. The likes of him helping you out is very different from consulting doctors, psychologists or professional counsellors of every type. It's no big deal for a surgeon, for example, to remove a painful appendix or swollen tonsils or to treat any other part of the

214

body that's a source of trouble to you. A painful conscience is something else altogether however!

Given that I had thousands of pounds on me at the time, I didn't mind parting with some of it in order to get some relief from my pain.

(Isn't life amazing? And the progress that has been made in medicine? The skills that surgeons and doctors and psychologists and psychiatrists have garnered over the years? You could walk the whole of Ireland today and you'd rarely meet anyone whose conscience is afflicting them—at any stage!

In my case, I went to see Dr Don'tmindit anyway. At the beginning of my initial session with him, he was inclined to minimize my guilt and the malice that'd accompanied it.

"I understand sir that you're worried about the damage you caused to the development of the Irish language but it's not advisable for any of us to blame ourselves too much for anything. You need to remember the damage being done to the language by people other than yourself. It's not good for anyone to be going around saying to themselves: 'I'm the worst person in the world.' I'd remind you of how much bad poetry is being written in Irish by university students today. Or the torture this ancient mode of communication experiences at the hands of various government departments on a daily basis."

"Or the many teachers who spent their entire lives fomenting hatred for the language in the hearts of young children?"

Well, that sort of talk was fine until he fully understood what was I'd done exactly. The more I explained the situation to him in detail however, the more his interest was piqued. And I could see by the way his eyes widened with surprise that his respect for me was only increasing. On realizing that I wasn't the usual type of blackguard that he had dealings with, his countenance changed. He was like the person who suddenly realizes that they are in the presence of a creature more cowardly than they are themselves. Dr Don'tmindit knew well that

215

he'd found someone who was entitled to be celebrated both far and near for his dedication to blackguardry. He realized that it was behind the most innocent and respectable of appearances that serious blackguardry and skullduggery always concealed itself.

He'd got an insight now into the type of personality someone required in order that they be cited in the annals of thuggery as an inspiration for the younger generations of reprobates coming through.

Once I'd finished telling him my woes, Dr Don'tmindit paced up and down the floor for a while forming his thoughts. It was clear that my story had had a big effect on him! In fact, I was afraid that he'd refuse to have anything to do with me and that I'd be back to square one and reliant on Father Givingout again—either that, or I'd have to get in touch with someone at a higher clerical level than him.

He didn't turn me down however. In relation to a problem such as yours Hassle, it's impossible to rely on hypnotism in the normal sense of the term because there is always a certain amount of the past that you can't wipe from your mind. It's like when the tide comes in across a wide, open beach. It covers everything except the big rocks and boulders that jut out above the level of the water. The issue at play here—is what do you do about whatever cannot be wiped from the mind, whatever cannot be transformed or changed and yet which is and which is unpleasant all the while? This is a problem that raises its head quite regularly in the ordinary course of life.

"Imagine a film or television actor preparing to step out into the glare of the bright lights—imagine an estate agent getting a new property ready for a potential buyer who wishes to view it—imagine someone trying to secure a reasonable price for an a battered, old car. In each of these cases, one seeks to direct the attention of the observer away from that which is ugly towards that which is more pleasing to the eye. The estate agent

PART 3 • CHAPTER 27

will build a new feature as part of the property. Plant some
trees maybe. Or construct a wall. Or make a garden to improve
the place and make it more beautiful. Film-makers, theatre-
directors, photographers, portrait painters or cosmetics' man-
ufacturers. They're always thinking of how the human appearance can be improved—by eliminating a worry-line here or
removing a shadow there etc. And as for the used car dealer
doesn't he try to play down whatever isn't attractive about the
product he's trying to sell. As the whole world knows!

You remember an incident in your past that continues to torment you and so the only thing to do is to source a credible
image from your subconscious, one that's happier and more
acceptable to your conscience—and eliminate that old spiky
and tarnished memory as best you can. Given that such mem-
ories can't be wiped completely clean, it's important to dream
up a beautiful, joy-filled series of images to replace those which
are ugly—to make of life a dream as it ought to be. Life as it
ought to be if every one of us had made the best choices in
every situation."

He shook hands with me as he accepted my cheque on the
way out. I didn't begrudge him the money one bit. £3,600
pounds, that was a hefty sum of money in Dublin back then.
But I'd have given him the same money again twice over for
the advice he gave me. So I came up with a much nicer memory
from my past, one that took the edge off things and brightened
up my day whenever life was gloomy or difficult.

Whatever I dreamed up didn't have to be real after all! It was
enough just to imagine it!

And that's how I've everything sorted out for myself now.
And also why there are two different endings to my story. It's
part of the treatment that Dr Don'tmindit laid out for me. Both
endings are there simultaneously, the happy ending and the
unhappy one.

I continued returning to Dr Don'tmindit for advice after this, paying for each session at the same rate I first gave him. Until his own health broke down that is. I believe that he's been in a mental institution now for years. And yet I'll be grateful forever to him. And I'll follow his advice forever too. Wasn't it he who saved me at the end of the day? And amn't I completely cured now nearly? Well, nearly completely cured—I've been taking it easy on the whiskey recently. I've been leaning more heavily on the barbiturates.

The Bad Ending

If what I did was an act of treachery, I'm not the first person in the history of humanity—or indeed, in the history of the Irish people—who did so. And don't imagine that I didn't make sure beforehand that it was worth my while. I was told very bluntly that my services were required. That I was valued and that I was needed. At the Disunited Nations, it was important that at least one of the Baroness' followers had their loyalty to her undermined. Otherwise, they'd never have managed to infiltrate and take over the Deutsch-Keltische-Stiller-Ozean-Genossen.

In matters of treachery, necessity is paramount. If there hadn't been a necessity for a Judas Iscariot, the thirty pieces of silver would never have been paid over—not even the fifteen pieces itself. In my own case, once I returned to Dublin, I never had to walk down the road and worry that I didn't have the price of a pint in my pocket. And I always had the price of a bus into town or whatever it cost to get to some social gathering or other. I could have spent the rest of my life cruising the world on an ocean liner.

The crux of the issue was that the Disunited Nations wanted to have La Isla Maldita—our golden island-Gaeltacht of the west—as a test centre for new methods of warfare and weaponry. What they wanted from us—the Deutsch-Keltische-Stiller-Ozean-Genossen—seeing as we'd crossed their path—was that the people living there wouldn't be transferred from there to anywhere else. It was far better in their view to observe the effects of the weapons on a living population. Once thing was for sure—no living creature would emerge alive from these weapons tests. The Disunited Nations had enough power and influence to keep this story out of the international media—or release it in a way that put a good spin on it for themselves—that side of things would've been very easy for them—especially if the Deutsch-Keltische-Stiller-Ozean-Genossen had never advertised its coming or goings to that same island.

It pains me to say this but my old friends and I fell out about all of this. And when you think of all we'd been through together. What good was that to me—that this was my final contact with them—and that any interaction I had with the group after this back in Ireland was a hostile one.

This wasn't how I'd wanted things to end between us—all nice and happy—(by then, it'd dawned on them how perilous the whole testing thing was)—I alone knew that everything had already been arranged, that it was a *fait accompli,* as the French say:

Sorley was the first of them to become suspicious of me—one day, he stared me straight between the eyes and says:

"It'd be easy to smuggle all these women back to Ireland, wouldn't it?" he says, "for the sake of the promotion of the language!" In my imagination, I saw O'Connell Bridge in Dublin lit up gold-red on an Autumn evening and a line of these South American women crossing the river one after another—I saw their patient stoic, dark-skinned-faces and their raven-black hair hidden beneath their bowler hats, each woman sporting a poncho—one woman with her child cosy and warm beneath her wrap while another carryied a rifle. The image disturbed me.

It wouldn't work. Ever since the Irish travelling people had given up speaking Irish the language movement had become more and more middle-class and the language was dying. Even if the language still existed to a certain degree it had become very-very *respectable* altogether.

"Bring them back to Ireland, to promote the language is it? You couldn't do that—Ireland wouldn't suit them at all—there'd be questions asked."

"Questions?"

"Oh, you know yourself! Questions around citizenship and visas—the veto—there'd be lots of "red tape" involved!

"I thought…" one of the Germans said, adding his tuppence-worth that Ireland was a country that always welcomes strangers!"

I was trying to imagine these women in such circumstances. And they speaking Irish! What would people say? So, I says to the German.

"A country of welcomes? Oh! Sure. Of course it is. Of course! We give everyone an incredible welcome! A hundred thousand welcomes! Bord Fáilte and all that!" And I left the group at this point. What was the use in me talking anymore?

In all honesty, I never experienced anything but kindness and gentleness on the part of these Irish-language activists—I have to say this—despite the awful things that people say about them—that they're all arms traders and weapons-dealers and the like…

So much so that they even organized a little party in my honour before I left! They were disappointed that I wouldn't wait to see the testing for myself. They could easily have arranged for me to observe the bombing trials from a safe place if I'd wanted to. But, as I explained to them, I was in a hurry to return to Ireland after all my various adventures abroad.

If you'd seen the type of people who turned up at that going-away party! There were at least three or four people there who were millionaires—between oil barons, mining executives, travel company and airline owners, the people who are wiping out the rainforests, bankers and politicians—every big-shot was there with glamourous women in tow. The place was crowded with senior army officers and military types, air force and naval officers included—all of them swanning around in their gleaming uniforms, gold-lace and brass buttons, and medals hanging out of them.

They all made a big deal of me and told me that my decision to return home was a courageous one—so much so that I nearly began to believe them myself after a while.

Deep down, I knew full well that I'd never have it in me to face the likes of Sorley or Maolchú or Brendan or the Foreign Professor or von Rumata ever again. Never mind von Volcaniceruption. Never mind Baroness von Wink.

One of the most important figures there said that the world would understand one day in the future that I had done the right thing—even if I myself would have preferred if the world never knew anything at all about the whole affair or my involvement in it either.

Later that night when he had a lot more alcohol on-board, the same man claimed that people would remember my actions until the end of the world—even if this didn't happen for another six or seven years!

The Good Ending

The good ending to this story, of course, is that we managed
bring all the bronze-skinned women from South America
back with us as immigrants to Ireland. And these same women
settled in Ireland, mixed in with the locals and their community has spread throughout the country ever since. They make
a living running small shops called *boliseanna*, a word that's in
common use in Bolivia and Peru, meaning a restaurant or café
but a type of café the likes of which had never been seen in Ireland prior to their arrival. On the menu in these cafés you find
vegetables such as Oca. Mashua and Ollucas. Also Húntó or
Chúiniú, a type of black-dried potato, Saltenas (a sort of a meat
pie). And Humintas (a dessert) and many smaller dishes such
as Iló Quinua maybe, or Empnada, or Pato, Gobida, Chur-
rasco, Vatapa, Tucupi, Gilo, Milagneto.

Seeing as here in Ireland, the people prefer big meals, you
might have a main course of Moqueta de Peixie or Xinkim de
Gallina in one of their cafés. As seasoning with such a meal,
you might request Locota (a form of pepper) or a hot sauce
known as Illojua or Jallpja Huaca. You might wash that down
with a cup of Maté de Bioca, a form of tea that's commonly
drunk throughout Latin America. And if it's an alcoholic drink
you require, they drink a type of beer called "Chicha." People
don't live on food alone, needless to say. Say now that you're
the type of person who isn't too bothered about their stomach

and you wanted to try something interesting besides food or drink while visiting one of the boliseanna? If you were lucky you might get to see a performance by a group performing the Comparsa or the dance known as the Huayno. There'd be musicians there playing on the Tarka and the Prinquillo too.

And once or twice I have heard that lonely music played on the instrument known as the "quena", the flute that's native to the Altiplano, the region containing tilled farmlands at the highest and most remote altitude in the world.

Here goes with a song belonging to the indigenous people of South America that I translated into Irish originally. It relates to the thoughts of a solitary guerrilla fighter who's on the run in the jungle. The guerrilla suggests here that he'd be safe from his pursuers if the forest birds didn't reveal his presence to the enemy.

As I stood in the jungle-thicket this morning,
The birds of the air rose up in flight:
They wouldn't let me go unnoticed.
Hidden in the thicket in the early-day,
I tried my best to go unseen
Even if the flight of the birds was an incredible sight
I thought they could have waited instead of scattering like this
Right there in my presence,
They could have just pretended not to see me
And not given away my hiding place so easily;
You'd have thought that they'd have done this much,
And abandon their feeding ground,
It would've been easier for them not to make a show
And to have ignored me instead
That would've been just a small favour to me
With my enemies coming after me,
Just as the bird escapes into the air
I too would rather not die rising out above the earth

And overcoming death forever!
Every flower eventually falls to earth
And the enemy is now close by
There's no harm going into battle
Even if it's always better to be alive!